Lessons We Leave Behind:

Meditations on a Father's Love Through His Son's Life Lessons

For a son who has gone ahead to heaven
and the 42 Life Lessons he left behind

Lloyd E. Dunlap

All Scripture references are taken from the New American Standard Version of the Bible.

Photograph of Christopher Charles Dunlap after receiving his white coat during a ceremony with his medical school. He went to be with the Lord 5 days later.

Contents

The Life Lessons from Chris

22. Don't make excuses for why someone else is successful and you are not.

23. Ask for advice on what the appropriate situation is. Try to select the most level-headed person to ask this.

24. In the classroom, don't stand out until you have a good feel for what is appropriate. Also, don't be a know-it-all at any point in time, ever. The quiet people don't like it.

Why Faith is Indispensable

25. Waiting often hurts a lot and leaves you lost in the woods. I have no idea what to expect tomorrow, next week, next month, but I still have faith.

26. Have faith that this is what God wants for you; especially when you are lonely.

27. Go to church and breathe deeply.

28. Believe in God. Although his plan may seem impossible, it is still a plan.

29. Today you've had your greatest accomplishment, thanks to the mercy of the Lord.

Managing Relationships While Managing Yourself

30. You never know how much some people care about you until you are heading away so cherish every moment.

31. Your greatest weakness is your temper. Even if it is unfair and it sucks- reacting badly will only hurt you.

32. Don't obsess over things you can't change.

33. Stay in contact with those who helped you in your journey.

34. Learn what makes someone mad and avoid it or try the things that help relieve it.

35. Be kind to those who may seem different from you or not as intelligent.

36. Forgive people, but also don't be mean to them.

37. Don't steer people in the wrong direction.

38. Don't ever try to get revenge.   If someone makes you mad, you have to let it go.

39. Don't judge others who are different than you and you do not know anything about.

40. Don't be a part of someone else getting hurt.

41. Try not to judge others. You haven't walked in their shoes.

42. Don't be arrogant or opinionated. Accept and praise other's opinions.

Dedication

When I told my wife, daughter and some good friends
about an inspiration to write this book, they encouraged me to
get started. Therefore, I dearly appreciate the accountability to
continue writing the book from my wife Cindy, my daughter
Lindsey and my friend Jim Reitz. I also appreciate the
encouragement from our new dear friend Wen Marcec. Wen
stayed with my son at the scene of the automobile crash as
he passed from life on earth to life in heaven. Finally, Mary
Lou Craig and Michael Hagood added great reviews and
recommendations for the book.

Preface

My son, Christopher (Chris) Charles Dunlap, died in a catastrophic automobile crash on September 29, 2010. He was a mere 30 years old. Many have experienced the loss of a child in life and all of us will one day experience the loss of someone dear. Death is part of life. We cannot escape it.

God alone knows what happened at the moment when Chris died in the automobile crash. God alone knows the reasons for what happened. Chris was in medical school studying to be a doctor. His goal was to serve the poor in a third world country. Just as God did not explain the reasons to Job in the Old Testament, God has never explained to me why this tragedy happened in my life. Someday in heaven, I will understand.

What I have written about in this book is the miraculous way God finally answered my prayers for my son before he died. However, God answered my prayers in a way I did not expect. In addition, the journey for the answered prayer was long and painful. We sometimes pray God will answer our prayers quickly and in ways we find pleasant. Answered prayer does not always happen this way. Just read the struggles and prayers of David in the Psalms. Likewise, read the struggles of Solomon and Job in the Old Testament and Paul in the New Testament.

In Psalm 23: 4, David talks about walking through a valley that is difficult, dark and dangerous. *"Even though I walk through the valley of the shadow of death, I fear no evil, for You are with me; Your rod and Your staff, they comfort me."* Even though God takes us through valleys that are painful, God promises He will lead and guide us through it. His comfort is available to us as we walk through these gloomy times. God's guidance through the valley is the right path and the safest path. Most importantly, God guides us on our walk "through" the valley and we will finally emerge on the other side. God does not keep us in the valley. He also never tells us when we will come out of the valley and reach our destination. Likewise, He does not tell us what the other side of the valley looks like.

As I emerged from the valley I can see the marvelous hand of God. He answered my prayers Chris would someday glorify God. After Chris died, I learned my son had reached a point in his life where he stepped out and openly glorified God and wanted to serve Him. God's path to my prayers' answers was not my plan. I would have preferred a path with less pain. However, I know God's perfect plan is, and always will be, the right one. His will and timing are perfect and it is always exactly what I need. I now know what God is doing is always best for me, even though I do not see it at the time. God never promised me He would explain His plan to me while I am here on this earth. As a human, I would not be skilled enough to understand it. Someday I will understand, but I believe I will likely have to wait until I am with Him in heaven.

Chris was an extreme challenge during his teenage years. My wife and I experienced years of pain with our son as a very rebellious young man. We raised both our children to love and obey the Lord. We took them to church activities, Christian family camps in the mountains of Colorado and read Bible stories to them at bedtime. We read dozens of highly recommended Christian parenting books and went to Christian parenting seminars. We even went to secular family counseling. We tried to model godly parents and godly character. But at the time, all this seemingly failed and seemed to crash down around us like a bridge suddenly gives way to the stress and finally collapses into the water.

The years when Chris was a teenager were some of the most stressful of my life. I was jealous of other parents who seemed to have well-behaved children. I would cry out to God. Wasn't I doing the same things as other parents in our church? Why did we have this grief and other parents had calm and obedient children? Why did God give this pain and suffering to us?

After Chris graduated from high school, I told him it was time for him to move into an apartment I would pay for. I thought the timing was right because he would be starting at the local university within the next two months. I had saved enough money to put him through college. Even though we thought this would make things better, Chris moving out of our home started the most painful period in our lives. When he moved out, instead of getting an apartment, Chris joined the Army and then did not speak to us or contact us for about three years.

During this time, I could not understand God. We had a son we nurtured for his first 18 years of life. We knew we had done the right thing in teaching him about the Lord and raising him in the church, but now we had lost him. He was out there in the world somewhere, but we literally had no knowledge if he was soldier serving somewhere in the United States or a soldier in harm's way in some hostile foreign country. We had no idea where he was or what he was doing. This caused agony that was excruciating. My wife and I would cry out to God at night.

During this time, my wife and I could only turn to God. Our refuge was in the Lord. Even though I prayed earnestly, seemingly no answers came from God. I constantly tossed through my mind what would have happened if I had not had him leave our home after graduation. What if I had been a better father? What if I had not moved the family to Kansas when he was in Junior High School? What if I had not forced him to go to church with us as a teenager?

My prayers became more simple and shorter because my long, eloquent prayers seemed futile. My prayers became simple because I was exhausted from asking God to have Chris return to Him. I felt I was not being heard. In the back of my mind it seemed hopeless that my prayers would be answered. God did not seem to be listening and my pain was so great. My continual prayer for Chris quite simply changed to: "Lord, have Chris glorify You someday".

The purpose of this book is to demonstrate God did answer my simple prayer to have Chris glorify God someday. I am also convinced He will also answer your prayers. In my case, He did not answer my prayer immediately, nor did He answer it the way I was expecting. God continued to take me through the pain of a lost son for several years, and of course, the continual pain today as a father who has experienced the death of a son.

What you will see in this book is how God answered my prayers. God transformed Chris, and as a result, God is also transforming me. God took my son on a journey not too unlike the journey of the prodigal son in Luke 15 in the Bible. Chris became a young man who demonstrated a deep faith in God, a faith he would share with others. It was like God said to me: "I told you I would answer your simple prayer".

In his later years, Chris himself wrote he wanted to "glorify God" in his life by becoming a doctor. In one of his applications to a medical school in California, Chris wrote his passion was to "*dedicate seven years of his life to become an International Medical Aide. He believed through the medical and spiritual guidance obtained at medical school, he could make a difference in the world by bringing God's Word to underserved populations and expanding the glory to our Savior.*"

Chris went on to write in this application "*he came to believe everything he achieved was through the grace of God. Even though he went through many tests and trials in life, his strength, determination and faith helped him believe the Lord was always there to help him grow in the walk through this adversity he once faced*'. He added he wanted to '*exemplify the true value in life is serving the Lord with a pleasant and willing heart and never giving up the battle on the mission they were given*'.

I now know God always has a perfect plan and I have no right or skill to understand it or question it. During these years, God was orchestrating His plan in Chris's life. Chris had marvelous experiences in his young life few of us will ever be able to taste. Even with his numerous friends and international travel, life for Chris during these years was never easy. Chris had both times of great blessings, marvelous friends and personal victories, and also times of deep agony, emotional struggles and loneliness. Like in Psalm 23:4, Chris was led by God through the valley on a spiritual and emotional healing that was slow but continual. Each Life Lesson found in this book will give you a glimpse into his life during this journey.

During the last years Chris had on earth, God was also answering my prayer, even though I did not see it at the time. In addition, through this period of time and even now, God is still working on me. I am the one who now understands "I" also need to glorify God in a manner similar to how Chris did. Through the way Chris lived his life and these Life Lessons, I am now better able to see what I need to do and how I need to do it.

In his early years when Chris was growing up, we were teaching him about life and following after God. But now Chris, the son, teaches me, the father, through these Life Lessons. Through these Life Lessons and their applications Chris is teaching me every-day lessons on how to love God, love my neighbor and value God's blessings. But most dramatically, Chris is teaching me how to visibly and practically live a life that honors and glorifies God and how to demonstrate and apply godly character in my own life. I hope in some way these Life Lessons will also teach you.

So I have come full circle. I prayed a simple prayer for Chris to someday glorify God. God answered my prayer. I want the reader to understand God will also answer prayer for you.

In the midst of the pain and grief I have experienced since losing Chris, I have never given up on God. After Chris died, instead of being angry, bitter or reacting badly and showing my pain in front of others, I have remembered to focus on God. Like Job, I should never take refuge or solace in my possessions, family, experience or wisdom. These can all disappear like the Kansas wind can change direction.

I recognize my faith in the Lord is the only thing I have to stand upon. Everything else will one day fade away. I cannot get angry and demand God give me an explanation on why Chris died. Because I know and trust God, I do not need to know the details of His plans. I do not need to know why Chris died at the age of 30 when his goal was to serve the Lord and the poor in a third world country. It is enough to know God loves me and He promises to guide me and comfort me. Likewise, He loves Chris and He still guides Chris and comforts him more than ever in heaven. I only need to remember God is in control, even when it appears He is not. I simply need to know and trust Him and rely on His promises. I am convinced I will see Chris again in heaven. Until that time, I need to demonstrate my love for God to others here on earth.

Origin of the Life Lessons from Chris

This book contains Life Lessons Chris wrote to himself on his laptop computer. Each Life Lesson we found is a phrase of a few words or sentence. When our daughter, Lindsey, found them on his computer after he died, we were astounded at their wisdom, perception and depth. With the backdrop of the journey in Chris's life and in my life, we have found these Life Lessons to be especially meaningful. We carry them around with us and contemplate what they meant to Chris. We have given out these Life Lessons to over one hundred people. To this end, this book is about providing you the Life Lessons Chris wrote. Each chapter of this book will start with the Life Lesson we found. Then with the help of my wife, Cindy, and my daughter, Lindsey, the family will provide the background and stories for what we believe the Life Lesson meant personally to Chris. Finally, we conclude each chapter with what Chris taught us personally through our difficult journey through life and how each Life Lesson is changing us.

It appears Chris wrote the Life Lessons during his last few years of life here on earth. He told no one about these Life Lessons and only Chris knew they existed. They are astounding when related to the friendships he experienced and the heart-wrenching tragedies from his personal journey through his 30 years of young life.

We think it fitting, as a tribute to Chris's life, to share these Life Lessons with you. If they help you, as they did us, we are sure Chris would not mind that we shared them. After all, helping others was what his life was all about.

This book was inspired by the Lord on February 20, 2011, while sitting at the Early Risers' Sunday School Class at First Baptist Church in Geneva, IL. This inspiration occurred while waiting for the class to start and I was looking at my Bible bookmark which listed Chris's Life Lessons. The inspiration was not audible, but I felt something stir my soul. I knew it was from the Lord.

This book was started on February 26, 2011, and was completed through prayer and support of others and by the grace of God.

The Beginning of a New Life at the End of a Young Life

It was September 29, 2010. It was the longest night of my life. I was in Seattle, Washington. I traveled quite a bit for my job with a large oil company. I had traveled throughout the country for years. I was typically gone from home one or two nights a week. Often I did this for 2 to 3 weeks out of the month.

The weather was beautiful in Seattle. I was having a nice dinner at a restaurant with my two colleagues from work, Vilia and Paul. Also with me was my long-time business associate and good friend from Seattle, Steve Wood. What a pleasant dinner it was. I recall Steve was a regular at the restaurant. He had been there many times and the restaurant staff knew him by his first name. Steve ordered for everyone without looking at the menu. He simply said to the waiter to bring whatever the chef suggested that night. I was impressed. I have been in thousands of restaurants over my life, but never had I ever simply asked the waiter to bring whatever the chef suggested.

I remember telling those at dinner table about my son Chris. He had just started medical school and I was so proud of him. I am sure anyone at the table could tell with the smile on my face when I spoke about him. Chris had moved in with us in our home in Geneva, Illinois, a small suburb 35 miles west of Chicago. Our daughter, Lindsey, had a good job and was living in Kansas. Before Chris moved in, Cindy and I were "empty nesters". It would be great to have him with us. And this would allow Chris to save on housing costs and commute to his medical school about 30 minutes away.

At the dinner table, we each talked about our families. Each of us spoke about where we were from and what we were doing outside of work. I was having a wonderful time. The food was excellent and the company of friends at the table was relaxing and pleasant. Life at that moment could not have been better. Cindy and I could have not been happier. My only son was going to medical school and I told most everyone. And most importantly, Chris, Cindy and I had reconciled with each other in the last few years. He was now living in our home after being away for 11 years. Cindy and I were elated.

The first few appetizers came to the table and everyone was relaxed and having an enjoyable conversation. Then my cell phone rang. I looked at the phone and it was my wife, Cindy. This was a bit surprising. Cindy usually did not call me when I traveled. I usually called her because I better knew the time I was off of work and able to talk. I had always made it a habit to answer calls from my family. I had been lovingly married to Cindy for 33 years at this time.

On the phone Cindy sounded nervous. She said a police car was parked at the curb in front our house. She went on to tell me she believed she had just seen a policeman come to the door and ring the doorbell. But before she could get dressed and come to the door, the policeman had gone away. She surmised the policeman had been looking for our neighbor directly across the street. This neighbor was a good friend and she was going through a terrible divorce. We had seen the police at their house recently. I told Cindy not to worry and see if she could get some sleep. Both Cindy and I hoped any problem would simply go away. This is what I wanted to think and I am sure Cindy wanted to think the same thing. After all, I was having a wonderful time at dinner.

About 10 minutes later my cell phone vibrated again and again it was Cindy. This time Cindy told me our next door neighbor and the policeman had just knocked on our door. The policeman was actually looking for us! Cindy told me on the phone, the policeman simply said to her Chris had been in an automobile accident and Cindy needed to come to the emergency room of the local hospital. The policeman did not tell Cindy how or if Chris was hurt, just that she needed to come to the hospital.

Instead of riding with the policeman to the hospital, Cindy wisely asked our neighbor if she would drive her to the hospital. Cindy had heard of stories how crazy men bought uniforms and impersonated police. Obviously Cindy was stressed at this point and she also wanted the company of our neighbor.

I also was now very worried, but I wanted to convey confidence and encouragement to Cindy over the phone. I told Cindy once she got to the hospital, to call me again and let me know how he was. Cindy agreed and then hung up.

I told my friends at the dinner table about the two phone calls and that my son had been in an auto accident. They wanted to know if I wanted to leave and return home. I told them I honestly I did not know if he had a few bruises, or if he was seriously hurt. I could make plans on what to do after I knew more of the story. So I recommended we go on with the dinner until I knew more details.

The Beginning of a Changed Life

The dinner continued, but my life was about to change forever. About 20 minutes later, Cindy called me again. I only could hear Cindy crying uncontrollably. I could not comprehend a word she was saying. I knew something was terribly wrong, but I did not know exactly what it was. I knew the news was not going to be good. Obviously, Chris had more than just bruises. Wanting to be able to hear and not disturb the other dinner quests, I got up from the dinner table and went to the front door of the restaurant where it would be a little quieter.

As I had walked the 50 feet to the front door I realized I was talking to our pastor, Roger Crites, at our church. Roger is a pastor's pastor, someone who put a smile on your face whenever you spoke to him. He is a very dear friend. Even though he was in a difficult fight with a tough cancer himself, he most often had a smile on his face and offered encouragement whenever you spoke to him.

As I was now no longer talking to Cindy, but to our pastor, my knees began to shake. Pastor Roger told me Chris was dead. Hoping I was still not hearing well due to the noise in the restaurant, I screamed back a question: "He is dead?" How many people in this restaurant heard me, I will never know. I sat down on a chair in the area where people were waiting to be seated. I was stunned. I did not know what to do. I could not wrap my arms around my wife. I had no one to hold me. I felt totally alone in a restaurant in Seattle.

After traveling for my job for over 20 years, my worst fear was being realized. A tragedy occurred at home and I was 2,000 miles away. I was helpless. I could not do anything or say anything to console my wife. I could not do anything to fix this. If you have ever traveled for business, you know what I mean. I never felt so alone. I am sure Cindy felt the same way. I did not even know how to pray, even though I knew I should. I simply had no words for God. I was not angry at God, but I simply did not know what to do. I was just numb.

Back on the phone, I had a period of silence that most likely lasted for a few seconds, but it seemed like minutes before I could talk again. I struggled to talk again to Pastor Roger. He went on to tell me Chris died an automobile crash in a Wal-Mart parking lot. He did not have details beyond that. I asked him to put Cindy back on the phone. All I could tell her was I was flying back that night. I had no words to comfort her. I knew and she knew when my wife needed me most in her life, I was out of town and helpless. I could not put my arms around her. I could not cry with her. I could not encourage her. I simply had no words. My mind was racing. Just how does someone die in an auto crash in a Wal-Mart parking lot? I could not get my mind around that. I knew I had to get home as soon as I could to be with Cindy.

I went back to the dinner table and went to the far side of the table where my friend Vilia was sitting. Vilia was my colleague I knew best. I knelt down next to her hoping not to have the entire table hear what I was going to say next. (Yeah, like I thought being inconspicuous was going to work!). I whispered to Vilia simply "My son did not make it". A look of terror came across her face and she began saying: "Oh Lloyd, No!", "No!" I do not remember what I said after that, I may not have said anything. Thankfully, those at the table started making decisions for me.

My friend Steve and his colleague agreed to drive me to my hotel to pick up my bag and then drive me to the airport. Along the way he arranged for a flight back to Chicago. The red eye! It departed around midnight and I would arrive back in Chicago O'Hare Airport at about 5:00 am.

We arrived at the hotel and I walked up to the registration desk. The hotel checked me out and did not charge me for the night. I simply told them a tragedy had occurred in my family and I had to leave. They did not ask me for details. I am sure they could see the look of despair on my face.

While riding in the car with Steve to the airport only a few words were spoken. After all, what does one talk about in a situation like this? Besides, I did not feel like talking. I could not get my mind around what had just happened.

I called my only daughter. Lindsey lived in Topeka, Kansas. She had lived in this area for years because most all of her friends were in Topeka. Cindy had simply asked me to call Lindsey and tell her about Chris. When Lindsey answered, I told her I had some bad news and Chris had died in a car crash this evening. I remember her saying, "No, c'mon dad". She thought I was joking. But in the back of her mind, I am sure she knew Dad would not joke about something like this. I told her again. The sobbing started and her life was now changed forever also. I asked her to pack some bags for an extended stay at our house and I would arrange for her to fly to Chicago that next day.

The Flight Home

Steve drove to the airport and took me to the United Airlines counter to get me checked in. He then walked me to the security lane. We all knew this was where we had to part. We gave each other a hug and I went through security. Now I was really alone. I felt alone before, but now my friends were no longer present. I was alone in the Seattle airport waiting for the flight back to Chicago. At a time like this, hundreds of thoughts race through your mind, none of which are helpful. With my science background, I am usually one who devises and analyzes a plan and then carries out the plan. All I knew was I needed to get on the jet and fly back home. After that I had no idea what would happen. I really did not care either.

Next was the longest plane flight of my life. Even though I had taken longer flights than this 4 hour flight from Seattle to Chicago, all I could do was stare at the back of the seat in front of me. I did not speak to anyone, I did not drink anything. I simply stared at the back of the seat. I kept asking to myself: "What was I going to do?" "What was I going to say to Cindy when I finally saw her the next morning?" I did not have a clue.

When I reached Chicago early the next morning, a car service was there to pick me up at the airport. It was still very dark outside. It normally took about one hour to reach Geneva from the O'Hare Airport in Chicago. I asked the driver to drive to my house a different way. I wanted him to drive me by the Wal-Mart parking lot where Chris had died. I had to see if I could make some sense of this. I was hoping for some answers.

The First Sign from the Lord

Along the way, something happened I will never forget. While staring out the window from the back seat of the car, I saw a large illuminated cross only about 100 feet off the road in the City of Elgin, Illinois. It was probably 25 ft high and it appeared so bright against the dark backdrop of the night. Still early in the morning and totally dark outside, it was the only light that illuminated the dark sky and surroundings. I thought the cross was likely hanging on the side of a dark building. But since everything else was still pitch black, I could not be sure. It seemed to be a bright, white beacon especially for me. I knew it was a sign from our Lord. This was the first feeling I had the Lord was with me. I know He had been with me all along, but this was the first time I felt His presence. He was telling me no matter how life was going to change for me, this cross let me know my son was now in the arms of Jesus. I stared back at the cross. It was so bright. I felt awe. I felt the beginning of a peace come over me.

I later learned this cross was hanging on the side of a church next door to the Westminster Christian School Chris attended when he was about 10 to 12 years old. Chris and Lindsey attended a Christian School in Elgin when Chris was in Junior High School and Lindsey was in Grade School. Cindy drove them each day from our home to the school. Chris and Lindsey loved that school. Since it was not a large school, Chris played soccer and basketball on the school teams. The teachers were great and caring.

Some may say seeing this illuminated cross next to Chris's former school was just a coincidence. But no one will ever convince me of that. This was my first sign from the Lord offering me comfort. When I did not know how to pray, He was telling me He was still there.

Finally Back Home

When I finally entered the door to our home, I first saw our neighbor who took Cindy to the hospital. She and her mother had slept on the couch and stayed with Cindy all night. Sadly, we had been having a spat with this neighbor for the last several weeks. We only spoke to say hello if we saw each other on the street or in the back yard. The spat did not seem so important now. Again, things were changing for me.

Cindy walked in from the bedroom when she heard me come in. I walked over to her and simply held her tight. I do not recall saying a word. There were simply no words to say. With all the answers and advice I had given her on how to fix issues and problems in our 33 years of marriage, I now had none. I began to cry for the first time since the phone call. The dinner in Seattle now seemed as if it was weeks ago. But in reality, it was less than 12 hours earlier.

And what did I see in the Wal-Mart parking lot the driver stopped at while driving home? I saw nothing. No crashed car, no broken glass, nothing. Life was now going to be this way. I had no answers. I did not understand. In fact, I am convinced I will never understand until the day I see Jesus. I may ask him. But then again, when I finally see the face of Jesus and my son, it will be so wonderful that whatever happened at Wal-Mart will not matter anymore.

Yes, I am positive I will be seeing my son again when I get to heaven. The letters, poems and Life Lessons he wrote to himself and to our Lord convinces me he now lives in heaven and I will see him again. The letters, poems and Life Lessons we later found while going through his things after he died convince me Chris had a close, personal relationship with our Lord. Some of his friends have told us how he shared his faith with them. So although he is gone now, it is just a matter of time before we see each other again.

A Changed Life

Life has changed for me. A few months after Chris died while walking with Cindy and doing Christmas window shopping in downtown Geneva, I read a poem in a small shop. It was a poem mounted in a frame one could hang on a wall. I read it over and over and then simply stared at it on the wall. Cindy continued to walk in the store, but the poem by Angela Schwindt just mesmerized me. It simply said:

> *While we teach our children about life,*
> *Our children teach us what life is all about.*

Chris wanted to give back to society and serve the Lord. He wanted to become a doctor in a third world country and serve those who could not help themselves. He did not want to become a doctor for the money, a big house, a fast car, or so he could golf during the week.

So my thoughts and passions began to change. I began to reflect on my life and what I was doing to serve the Lord and reach out to the world. Chris had so little in life, but he wanted to give everything he had, even his life to serve others. What was I doing? I realized I needed to humble myself and serve others also. Suddenly, my pride and desires to excel at work were not so important. Like Chris had done for years, I now needed a plan for my life to give back to serve others. I began to think about world missions rather than advancement at work.

I mentioned the first sign the Lord showed me when I saw the illuminated cross. But two other signs from the Lord occurred. One week after he died we had a memorial ceremony at the local cemetery at my home town where I grew up in South Haven, Kansas. We buried part of Chris's ashes there because most of the family members are buried at this cemetery. The cemetery is one mile off the main highway along a narrow, dusty dirt road. After the ceremony was over, I looked up into the sky and a large bird was circling overhead. It was so large either it was a Brown Eagle or a very large hawk. The significance of this is Chris loved eagles. His password and email address had the word "eagle" in it. He often talked about how free and spectacular they were. He hated to see them in a zoo because they were caged.

I motioned to Cindy and pointed to the eagle. Without saying a word, we both knew instantly this was another sign from the Lord. We turned to each other and smiled. Our simple look at each other said everything. No words were needed. Chris was with Jesus. Someday, we will see him again.

A few months later, Cindy and I visited the cemetery again. Understandably, we were both were still in pain from the loss of Chris. As we were leaving the cemetery and driving down the lonely dirt road, what appeared to be the very same bird flew alongside our car. The bird seemed to be the same one we saw earlier and it was about 100 feet away from our car and about 30 feet off the ground! And in our amazement, it flew alongside our car for what seemed to be about 30 seconds. Finally, it was gone as it flew into the trees along a small creek. Again, without saying a word, Cindy and I looked at each other and knew this was another sign from the Lord. Our son was free and happy. Our Lord wanted to give us another blessing and demonstrate everything was fine with Chris.

The Life Lessons
Enhancing Friendships

Chapter 1

Chris: Don't encourage your friends to do the wrong thing.

Chris was a natural leader and many people followed him. He became a Sergeant in the Army earlier than most he served with. Chris recognized his leadership skills and knew some people would follow after him, even if he was taking them down the wrong path. Therefore, he wanted to make sure he was a positive influence on people and not a negative one.

Chris believed a true friend would not let his friends get into trouble. Consequently Chris would speak out for his friends, but also confront his friends when needed. He would give them the correct perspective and not be afraid to tell them how to change their ways. Chris expected a lot from his friends and he expected even more from himself. In many ways, Chris was a father-like figure to his friends. He would tell his friends what they needed to be doing and how to do it.

And what his words mean to us

We should think back if we have ever had a friend who led us down the wrong path. Have we ever had a friend who was a bad influence or encouraged us to do the wrong thing? If we are honest, many of us have had friends like this at least one time in our lives. The key is to recognize it quickly and turn to find new, better friends.

If we lead others to do the wrong thing, we share in the responsibility of their actions. If we lead people to do the wrong thing, we share in their guilt. Chris taught us we have a responsibility to our friends to encourage them and build them up. Building them up is not flattery. It only comes from honest caring for their needs. And in order to care for their needs, we need to spend enough time with them to find out what their needs are.

We need to influence our friends for the better and keep our friends accountable. Friendship involves more than just getting together, playing golf or racket ball and having a good time. We need to be there when a friend needs us and we need to encourage our friends to do the right thing. We need to be a positive influence on them. This takes time and effort and it only comes from a deep and earnest caring for our friends.

When I lived in Geneva, Illinois and in Lawrence, Kansas, I met with close friends on Saturday mornings for breakfast. We had accountability questions we asked each other each Saturday. These questions were:

- How many times did you read the Bible this week?
- How many times did you pray with your wife this week?
- How many times did you exercise this week?
- Did you have any impure thoughts this week?
- Are you lying about any of your answers to these questions?

During the week I would remember I was going to be asked the five questions on Saturday morning. These questions made us accountable to each other and encouraged us during the week to read the Bible, pray, exercise and keep our thoughts pure. We are only doing a part of our responsibility when we advise our friends to not *do the wrong thing*. Our primary responsibility is to encourage them to do the right thing. This is what friends are for.

> *Therefore encourage one another and build up one another, just as you also are doing. I Thessalonians 5:11*

Chapter 2

Chris: Be a better friend to your close friends.

Chris knew how to be a good friend. After he died, so many of his close friends expressed how great a friend Chris was to them. He was funny and made his friends laugh. Chris was known to encourage his friends to become all they could be. He constantly watched out for his friends and was there when his friends needed him. He would go out of his way to help them.

Chris also made a point to stay in contact with his old friends. Chris did not take his close friends for granted. He knew he needed to cherish these friends because truly good friends are rare. He kept notes on what was happening in their lives so he could ask them about how these issues were progressing. He knew he should continually and outwardly show how he cared for his friends. Even though Chris spent so much of his time studying in college and for his medical school exams, he reminded himself not to be so consumed in his studying and work that he forgot about his close friends.

Later in his life, we saw a side of Chris his family never really experienced. He was often the "clown" in the group of his friends. Around his close friends he was extremely outgoing and the life of the party. Chris found a way to just be himself and enjoy being with his friends.

Cindy and I only briefly experienced this side of him. In the summer of 2010, we visited Chris in Colorado Springs. He had just completed his MCAT exams and received a good score. We went with him and his girlfriend to a piano bar in Colorado Springs. We had a wonderful time and the "crazy" side of Chris emerged for a few hours. I pulled out my camera to get a photograph of Chris and Cindy. Just before I clicked the camera for the photo, Chris quickly wet his finger and stuck it into Cindy's ear. The resulting photo shows a grimace on Cindy's face, but Chris had the biggest, brightest smile on his face. The contrast in their faces tells the story. We will cherish this photo forever. For a moment, we got to see Chris as the clown. This photo is so meaningful we displayed it at his memorial service and we now have it hanging on our wall at home.

Chris was known to listen carefully to his friends. He did this to pick up on things they said so he could later meet a particular want or need in their life or do one special thing they had mentioned. He would pay attention to these special details in their lives to show them how much he cared for them. This was his special way in helping his close friends. Chris would set aside his wants or needs and instead try to meet the desires of his friends. Some of his friends had more wants and needs than others; we all have friends like this. But Chris would always put out the extra effort to meet these extra desires, just because they were his friends.

And what his words mean to us

One has to understand what it means to be a *better friend*. Some of us have never felt we were very good at being a good friend. Chris taught us and gave us an example of how to be a close friend to someone and to encourage them. It takes time to be dedicated to being a friend and diligence in keeping up with those friends, even though they may no longer live close to you.

Even though we have moved away from friends, we need to make the effort to stay in close contact with them. We need to call people to maintain those friendships and even visit them whenever we can. If we do not stay in close contact, we will soon lose those valued friendships. We cannot just lay back and wait for those old friends to come and reach out to us. Unfortunately, this is exactly what we too often do in our lives.

The key is to *"be a better friend"*. We need to reach out to others we are only mildly acquainted with. Having just moved to Houston in 2011, Cindy and I have so many of these types of friends at our church we are only mildly acquainted with. It is so easy to simply say hello to them as we pass by on Sunday mornings. But this is not the type of friendship Chris was talking about. Being a *better friend* is so much more than a short conversation as we are passing by.

The value of encouraging friends often goes unnoticed. This is because we often encourage our friends privately when they feel most alone. When our friends feel most alone is the exact time when a close friend needs to come alongside them and give them the encouragement they need. Everyone needs encouragement at one time or another. We need to be drawn to people who need encouragement from us. If we can encourage them, we can also be a great help to them. If we stay close to them, we can then better pray for them and be available to them in the ways they really need to be helped. And to be successful in encouraging them and helping them, we need to start by *"being a better friend"*.

> *22 The news about them reached the ears of the church at Jerusalem, and they sent Barnabas off to Antioch. 23 Then when he arrived and witnessed the grace of God, he rejoiced and began to encourage them all with resolute heart to remain true to the Lord ; 24 for he was a good man, and full of the Holy Spirit and of faith. And considerable numbers were brought to the Lord. Acts 11:22-24*

Chapter 3

Chris: Try to re-establish friendships.

Chris had many friendships. However, during one low point in his life, he stopped connections with many of his friends so he would not have to face them. At the time, Chris did not understand his friends could have helped him through his pain and loneliness. Chris did not realize how much his friends cared for him and accepted him.

In 2009, Chris began to reestablish the friends he had left. His friends were eager to have Chris once again back in their lives. Chris realized he did not need to let painful circumstances continue to get in the way of those who he cared for. Chris understood he left his friends for the wrong reasons and he should not have turned away from those who were most important to him. This must have taken a great deal of humility.

And what his words mean to us

Dear and cherished friends are profoundly important to keep for our well-being. Some of you may have moved once or twice or even many times. Each time, you have likely left many good friends behind. Do not forget your friends after you have moved away. Keep those friendships or restore those relationships if you have lost contact. Be diligent in calling them, writing them and reconnecting with them. Do not forget about those friends with whom you spent so much time. It is not hard to re-establish lost friendships. Like this Life Lesson says, we need to "*try*". What a blessing this will be!

> *For if either of them falls, the one will lift up his companion. But woe to the one who falls when there is not another to lift him up. Ecclesiastes 4:10*

Chapter 4

Chris: Try to be a better friend to people.

C hris was the ultimate example to being a great friend to people. This Life Lesson was not only to be a *friend to people*, but Chris wanted to be a "*better*" *friend to people*. This is a Life Lesson to be constantly improving on reaching out to others and being an excellent friend.

Chris went above and beyond to be a great friend. He made this a priority in his life. He took pride in how many unique and novel things he could do for his friends. He gave small affordable gifts to his friends, for no other reason than they were his friends and he knew it would make them happy. Chris put the interests of his friends above his own. After he died, his friends poured out great memories of him and what a good and loving person he was. Obviously, Chris was very successful being "*a better friend to people*". He was loved by so many. We wonder from up in heaven if he could view his Facebook® page and see the loving memories of what his friends said about him after he died.

This is also a lesson about not holding back on meeting new people plus deepening the relationships with current friends. Chris did not settle to have only surface relationships with people. Chris wanted to have meaningful and mutually-giving friendships. These kinds of friendships take work and perseverance. They take time to develop and nurture. They take a pouring out of yourself. But these are the kinds of friendships well worth the time because of the rewards of having wonderful, long-lasting relationships.

And what his words mean to us

We may never be as good a friend as Chris was. But for many of us, we need to do much better. We need to reach out more to people. We may have many casual relationships with those at our church and at our work. Although there is nothing wrong with this, this is not what is meant to be *"a better friend to people"*.

To be a *"better friend"*, we need to take an interest in their personal lives. We need to find out what makes them happy and what makes them sad. We need to discover the happy things going on in their lives, and also the hurts and sorrows they are experiencing. Only in this way, can we be *a better friend* and reach out to meet their needs. We can share and celebrate with them when they are celebrating. We will be there for our friends when they need us, help our friends when they need help, encourage our friends when they need encouragement and care for their interests ahead of our own. Similar to Chris, we can give small gifts to show our appreciation for them and take them on small fun trips just to be with them. If they live a long way from our home, we need to make arrangements to reach out to them and talk with them.

If we apply these characteristics from this Life Lesson, we will have the same types of friends in our lives Chris made so much effort to keep in his life. And when we die, those friends will be as loving and thankful for us for being part of their life, similar to the feelings Chris's friends had during his life. We had better get started!

> *So, as those who have been chosen of God, holy*
> *and beloved, put on a heart of compassion,*
> *kindness, humility, gentleness and patience;*
> *Colossians 3:12*

Chapter 5

Chris: Be a good influence on your friends; not the other way around.

Chris learned leadership qualities in the Army where he quickly rose to the rank of Sergeant. After the Army, Chris was conscious of others watching him to see how he would handle difficult situations. Chris always wanted to steer others in a positive way. He encouraged them to be the best they could be. He chose to see the qualities in people, no matter what others said about them.

After his death, the family received numerous stories from his friends about how they appreciated his encouragement and wise counsel. When Chris saw his friends being influenced in the wrong way, he would speak up and try to correct the situation. He wanted to influence others and show them how to make wise choices. Chris took pride in mentoring others to show how they could become a better person. He wanted to demonstrate how to care and serve others.

And what his words mean to us

We have often heard the saying: "What would Jesus do?" Jesus Christ is our perfect example in demonstrating how to love and nurture others. Being like Christ should be our desire. Christ called us the "*light of the world*". The symbol of the "light" is that it will stand out for others to see us. But we can hide our light when we ignore others, go along with the crowd and remain quiet when we should speak up.

Many of these Life Lessons follow precepts which are, or are similar to, truths found in the Bible. These Life Lessons show us how Chris applied truth to his own life. Now, these Life Lessons can be a comparison of precepts and truth which can be applied in our own lives. For example, what kind of influence are you on your friends? We can be a good influence on our friends, or we can be a bad influence. We can even have no influence on our friends when we choose to be silent when they are making poor decisions.

> *14 "You are the light of the world. A city set on a hill cannot be hidden; 16 "Let your light shine before men in such a way that they may see your good works, and glorify your Father who is in heaven. Matthew 5: 14, 16*

Chapter 6

Chris: Try your best to be a good friend to those who have accepted you as you are. They don't come along too often.

We all want to be accepted by others. We all want to fit in.
Chris knew he was older than most of his friends. Since
he served in the Army, he was generally 5 to 8 years older than
many of his friends at school. Rather than graduate from college
at age 22, he was 29. Chris was 30 in medical school when most
of his classmates were 23 or 24. Chris felt like he was a generation
apart. Even though Chris was intelligent, handsome and athletic,
he had trouble accepting that he fit in with his friends. Therefore,
Chris appreciated his friends who accepted and embraced him.
Chris felt valued by these friends because he did not feel judged by
them.

Chris wanted everyone, no matter who they were, to feel welcome and included. Chris was friendly to most anyone he met. He would also openly accept and include those who were friends with his friends. This is how Chris wanted to be treated so this is how Chris treated others.

And what his words mean to us

By the grace of God, each of us is different from the other. Each of us will have different opinions on certain issues. The key is to glorify God by demonstrating love to others, no matter who they are, what they look like, what they say, or what they do. When we do not accept others, we often demonstrate selfish behavior and try to please ourselves. We elevate our own lofty opinions and our own self-centered wants. We do not want to associate with those different from us.

We need to be like Christ and try to be more accepting of others. This does not mean we need to agree with everyone and embrace their beliefs or behaviors. Christ endured and was patient with all kinds of different people. Just read the stories of how Jesus Christ accepted others. Christ visited the home of Zacchaeus who was a hated tax collector, he demonstrated love and forgiveness to a scorned prostitute who was about to be stoned, and he openly communicated God's love with a foreign Samaritan woman at a well. With so many distinct people in this world, it is easy to become selfish and opinionated about others who act differently or have different beliefs. Since Christ accepted us for who we are, we need to accept others. This will bring glory to God.

> *Therefore, accept one another, just as Christ also*
> *accepted us to the glory of God. Romans 15:7*

Chapter 7

Chris: Realize who are your friends and those who are not, try harder to be nice to them. They will be hurt if you don't give them a chance.

C hris tried hard to be nice and pleasant to even the most difficult people he knew. When Chris sensed a disagreement or a confrontation with someone, he made the extra effort to reach out to them. Chris wanted to learn more about them to understand and determine the source of the tension. He did not want to give up too quickly on a friendship. Chris wanted to resolve the issues and restore a friendship.

In this Life Lesson Chris also added: "*They will be hurt if you don't give them a chance*". He was especially concerned with those who were hurting and the feelings of others, even those who were not his friends. He wanted to encourage those who were outcast or were less popular. He wanted them to feel valued and special in their own way.

And what his words mean to us

We all need to deal with difficult people. First we need to love them and come alongside them in patience and kindness. We need to give our hearts to them, and expect we may not receive anything back in return. We need to be humble in spirit toward them.

Most importantly, we need to pray. First, we need to pray for ourselves because it is likely we also need to change our hearts and minds toward a difficult person. Do we ourselves have an unforgiving attitude toward them? We need to pray we will have compassion for others who are hurting inside and be taught how we can reach out to restore the relationship.

Secondly, we need to pray for those who are difficult. They need the same love, grace and mercy we have received from the Lord.   At the cross, our Lord forgave those who put him there (Luke 23: 34). Therefore, we need to imitate the humility, love and compassion Christ had. This kind of response to difficult people will be pleasing to the Lord.

> *The Lord's bond-servant must not be*
> *quarrelsome, but be kind to all, able to teach,*
> *patient when wronged, II Timothy 2:24*

Good Character in a Modern Age

Chapter 8

Chris: Try to stay away from a wicked tongue that speaks ill of others.

Chris's Life Lesson is so similar to what Job in the Old Testament would have said. Even with all the tragedies in Chris's life, he always wanted to see the best in people. Job wanted to follow God's way of living. Chris did also. Chris knew he was not perfect. Therefore, he did not want to criticize others.

As Chris became older, he thought before he spoke. He also did not want to talk about others behind their back. He saw the harm and damage from gossip. Chris would remind people he personally knew how hurtful gossip could be.

Chris wanted to see the positive and try to make the best of a bad situation. That included making every effort to not being critical of others. We think he saw that he, like all of us, had his own faults.

<u>And what his words mean to us</u>

Far too often we are critical of others. We should understand encouraging others, rather than being critical, is far better. After he died, many of Chris's friends told us how he encouraged each of them. It seems so simple the more you encourage your friends, the more friends you will have. The more friends you have, the more influence you have on people. And the more influence you have on people, the more you will have the ability to share your faith and lead them to a walk with the Lord.

It is easy to be critical of others, while ignoring our own faults. Before we criticize others, we need to check to see if we also deserve the same criticism. Chris was saying to take a look at ourselves before we speak ill of others. Chris taught us we should reach out to others and lovingly help them and encourage them.

> *3 For as long as life is in me, And the breath of God is in my nostrils, 4 My lips certainly will not speak unjustly, Nor will my tongue mutter deceit.*
> *Job 27: 3-4*

Chapter 9

Chris: Do not lie about anything to anyone. Work on developing a well-honed conscience and awareness of your surroundings.

Chris was incredibly honest. As his parents, we do not recall him lying to us in his later years. Chris wanted to be honest with everyone. In this Life Lesson, he obviously strove to *"not lie about anything, to anyone"*.

We recall one time while Chris was in high school we understood he was going to an all-night "lock in" at our church. We were happy he was going to spend time with his Christian friends and be around the church youth leaders. We found out a few days later he had not gone to the church, but instead he went to a party at a friend's house. When confronted, he did not lie to us. He readily admitted it.

In his later years, Chris came back to walk with the Lord. And when Chris did, he sought to have the virtues of a godly man. He saw these virtues of not lying and he wanted a godly conscience.

He sought the Lord in his own way. One could tell he wanted to serve the Lord. We think this was what he was referring to in this Life Lesson when he wanted to *"work on developing a well-honed conscience"*. Chris wanted to serve others. While at Chaminade University he wanted to raise money for the victims of Hurricane Katrina. He also raised money for the Premananda Orphan Center in India.

We are not quite sure what he meant in his Life Lesson about *"awareness of your surroundings"*. It may have been Chris wanted to appreciate what he had. Chris was not materialistic. He could and did live with very simple things. He never drove a sporty new car or had classy clothing. Chris wanted to keep his surroundings very simple.

Chris also made it a priority to help his friends. He wanted others to enjoy life and live life with a smile. He dearly wanted to be a positive influence on his friends. He wanted to mentor others and take care of those who were lonely, depressed or had low self-esteem. After he died, we heard numerous stories from his friends about how he went out of his way to look for these people and come alongside of them.

At his service at Punchbowl National Veterans Cemetery, one of his Hawaiian friends named Lance told us Chris took a group of friends on a difficult hike. Lance was lagging behind because he was new to hiking and not in very good shape. Chris, who was leading the group, intentionally slowed the others down and went to the rear to walk with Lance. This was another example of Chris being *"aware of his surroundings"* and noticing someone who needed help.

At one time while he was studying for his medical school exams, he lived with his sister Lindsey in Topeka, Kansas. Chris tried to mentor and encourage Lindsey. Chris believed Lindsey was hanging out with the wrong kind of friends. As a result her motivation to finish college was suffering. Chris did his best to encourage Lindsey to seek new friends and he tried to lift her spirits.

These examples show Chris was not only applying this Life Lesson to him, but also to others.

And what his words mean to us

Our lives need to be full of integrity. What we say to others will give them a window into our lives. If others perceive we are lying to them, our witness for the Lord is hypocritical. They will see we are no different from anyone else in this fallen world.

Chris went on to say to "*work on developing a well-honed (or razor-sharp) conscience*". Just as what we say to others gives them a window into our lives, our conscience gives God a window into our mind and our thoughts. We can hide our thoughts from others, but we cannot hide our thoughts from God.

In Romans 12:2, Paul told us to be transformed by the renewing of our mind. It is so easy to conform to this world with its selfishness, materialism and low morality. Chris referred to this as our "*surroundings*" in this Life Lesson. He added we need to "*work*" to prevent our minds and our conscience from being conformed to this world. When we transform our mind, we must fill our mind with thoughts from the Lord. To accomplish this, we must let the Holy Spirit renew and redirect our thoughts. Only then can we continually be transformed to the man or woman Christ wants us to be: full of integrity, living as a man or woman of God and a Christian testimony to others. This is not a once in a lifetime event. Renewing our mind and having a well-honed conscience takes day to day effort. Like Chris said, we must "*work*" at it; and we think he meant every day.

> *Do not conform to the pattern of this world, but*
> *be transformed by the renewing of your mind.*
> *Then you will be able to test and approve what*
> *God's will is—his good, pleasing and perfect*
> *will. Romans 12: 2*

Chapter 10

Chris: Don't play games with your love.

C hris was a loving person to many and he was especially devoted and loyal when he was in a relationship with a woman. Chris earnestly believed he needed to be totally honest with any woman he was dating and not play games with her heart. Chris would not be in a relationship just because he wanted a companion. He felt devotion was critical to the relationship. He did not want to take advantage of someone who loved him. He felt if he played games with his love, he would not only hurt the other person, but he was setting himself up to be hurt.

Chris wanted to be truthful and upfront with his relationships. Commitment to a woman was a slow process for Chris because he did not want to lead someone on. He took his relationships very seriously. Therefore, he stayed faithful and did not sneak around their backs and pursue other relationships.

A relationship with a woman was a partnership to him; not a game to win. It meant sacrificing his wants to honor the other.

Possibly the greatest quality Chris had was his deep commitment to whatever he did. He spoke of commitment often. Chris was separated from his girlfriend during the time he stayed with us in 2010, but his commitment never waned. Rather than go out on a date with another woman, he would often just stay at home and study.

And what his words mean to us

True dedication to a relationship takes dedication and commitment, whether it is our love for the Lord or our love of our spouse. We need to be honest with our spouse and never deceive him or her. We need to be loyal and honor them above all others. We need to show a strong affection for them. We need to show our delight and pleasure to be with them. We need to honor them and ensure they are contented and satisfied. We need to protect them from hurts, injuries and abuses. We need to provide for their needs. We need to demonstrate our love to them in private and also demonstrate it to them in public. We need to give them our total devotion. We need to communicate with them openly and often about our commitment. We need to be open with them on what is on our mind. We need to make sure we do not withhold our love or threaten to take it away from them. Finally, we need to spend time with them.

> *Husbands, love your wives, just as Christ also loved the church and gave Himself up for her,*
> *Ephesians 5:25*

Chapter 11

Chris: Don't steal.

Today many believe stealing is acceptable and justified, especially when the economic times are so difficult. Chris acknowledged the temptation of stealing exists in today's society. He never wanted to justify stealing, no matter how much he desired to have something. Chris knew in his heart stealing is never acceptable to the Lord. It is Satan who puts temptation in our sight and makes stealing enticing. Chris recognized he must resist this temptation and taking the easy way of getting something free.

And what his words mean to us

Stealing is more than just taking an item from a store. Even when your financial situation allows you to afford most everything you need, stealing can take other forms. For example, we need to continually challenge ourselves to be completely honest and forthright with our employer. Do we put in the hours expected?

Do we fill out our travel expense forms honestly? Do we spend and treat the company money like it is our own?

It can happen in our spiritual life also. Are we returning the blessings the Lord has given us? Are we faithful in giving our tithe to the Lord, or do we justify we need to keep it for ourselves? We should be constantly asking ourselves: "what would the Lord want me to do?" We should never justify in our mind to take something or keep something because the Lord would want us to have it. We should never believe it is acceptable for us to have something for ourselves that really belongs to the Lord. It is possible Satan may be enticing us or trying to convince us we deserve it. We need to fight those desires and thoughts.

> *13 Let no one say when he is tempted, "I am being tempted by God "; for God cannot be tempted by evil, and He Himself does not tempt anyone. 14 But each one is tempted when he is carried away and enticed by his own lust. James 1:13-14*

Chapter 12

Chris: Don't cheat on the person you're with. Don't help someone else cheat.

Chris was faithful to his girlfriends. He went to great lengths to show honor and remain true to them, even when they were sometimes separated by long distances. After he died, girlfriends told us how considerate and respectful he was. Chris believed remaining faithful to his girlfriend was a badge of honor. He often spoke how sad it made him when he saw his own male friends cheating on their girlfriends. It seemed to be consistent with his character of not wanting to hurt another person.

Chris had several friends and many of them were women. He wanted to be very honest with his women friends by letting them know if he was looking for a relationship or he simply wanted a good friend. He did this to let them know of his intentions and not send the wrong signal.

Chris never had a lot of money in his young life, but he prided himself in innovative ways to show his girlfriend a wonderful time on dates. He would come up with novel, small gift ideas. Chris would listen for small hints from his girlfriends and then he would provide a gift to match the want or desire. He loved to surprise his girlfriends by hosting a small party. Chris would cook gourmet meals for his girlfriends, and sometimes even for his mother.

We learned of daytrip dates such as a hiking in the mountains, kayaking to remote islands off Hawaii, and visiting small tourist towns in the Colorado Rocky Mountains. All this was done to show his honor, devotion, commitment and respect for the woman he was dating. Cheating on her likely never entered his mind. He would have made a great husband.

And what his words mean to us

We need to treat our loved ones with love and devotion. We need to treat them with the honor and respect they deserve and as our partner in life. A great example of how we should love our spouse is how Jesus Christ loves His church. Jesus gave His life for the church. Just as Christ gave up everything for the church, nothing we have should be held back from our loved ones and our love should be without limits. We need to consider their feelings and needs above our own.

We need to continue to "date" our spouses. For many of us who have been married for many years, it is so easy to start coasting and sit at home. We need to look for fun things to do with our spouse to show them our earnest desire just to be with them. We need to look for small, exciting daytrips we both would enjoy. It will likely not be kayaking to a remote island off Hawaii, but we can find something wherever we are. We need to listen to them for those small signals to learn how we can surprise them with a small gift. We need to encourage them, rejoice with them when they are happy and come alongside them when they are hurting. Plainly stated, we need to show them how they still excite us. We need to show our spouse our life revolves around them and we want to please them every day until one of us goes to be with the Lord.

> **18** *There are three things which are too wonderful for me, Four which I do not understand : **19** The way of an eagle in the sky, The way of a serpent on a rock, The way of a ship in the middle of the sea, And the way of a man with a maid. Proverbs 30:18-19*

How to Best Serve Your Fellow Man

Chapter 13

Chris: Be love, show love, accept love, and do not let the cold winter winds drag you to dark places. You have been given a gift and you are the most blessed person on this earth, so you need to show people that.

Chris was loved by many, but he may have had a hard time believing this. The standards he set for himself were so high and his desire and drive to succeed were great. He may or may not have realized the great blessings he was given by the Lord. He may have been surprised about the outpouring of the people who told us how they loved Chris. His *Facebook* ® page quickly filled with testimonies and stories of how he touched so many lives. People were in shock and deeply saddened to hear of his death.

Chris showed love and kindness to all he knew. Showing love to others motivated him. He not only reached out to those he knew well, but he reached out to those who he barely knew. He watched for those who might be hurting, feeling lonely, or feeling unappreciated. Chris knew he was blessed and wanted others to feel they were worthy and good. Chris truly considered the interests of others more than his own interests. He cared so much for people and he had high expectations for people. His friends told us few others cared for others as much as Chris did.

Chris wanted to inspire others to be better and achieve all they could achieve in life. He also knew he needed to do this for himself. Chris understood if he isolated himself from others, he would become depressed. When Chris closed himself off from others, he indeed felt lonely and he felt the world was cold around him. By inspiring others, Chris motivated himself and brought himself out of feeling lonely. Chris felt his worth by helping others.

By the grace of God, Chris realized his dream and was admitted into medical school in the summer of 2010. Chris became a first-year medical student at the Chicago College of Osteopathic Medicine at Midwestern University in Des Plaines, Illinois. He received his traditional "white coat" in a ceremony at the Rosemont Convention Center in Chicago just a few days before he died.

While we were going through his things after he died, we noticed several collapsible umbrellas in his room. These were not expensive umbrellas, but he had collected several of them. We later learned he bought these at a local dollar store and he intended to give these out to students at the campus of his Medical School who were caught in the rain without an umbrella. We do not know if he ever had the opportunity to give one away. But it demonstrated each of us can encourage others and reach out to others in small but meaningful ways.

In one of his medical school classes, each student was asked to write his obituary. Chris was the first student to be willing to read what he wrote in front of the class. His last line in the obituary was: "*live life with a smile, for what other way is there to live*". This saying is now on his cemetery grave marker in South Haven, Kansas. Chris was always aware life could be hard, but he did not want life to drag him down. He did not want to "*let the cold winter winds drag (him) to dark places*".

<u>And what his words mean to us</u>

Chris truly thought more of others than he did himself. Later in his life, Chris was the model of humility. He simply thought of others more than himself. How we wish we could remember that. He wanted others to feel good about themselves. Jesus Christ said the greatest command is to love God (Matthew 22:37). Jesus Christ went on to say the second greatest commandment is to love your neighbor (Matthew 22:39). Chris modeled for us how to do both.

We need to concentrate on what we can do to show love to God and show love to others. Like Chris, we need to encourage others and we need to reach out to others. It is easy to go along in life and be friends with those who are like us. We need to show love to those whom no one wants to be around or to those whom no one wants to touch.

Chris taught us how simple things can show love to others in a very meaningful way. He simply bought inexpensive umbrellas to share with strangers in need. We need to start thinking of others more than ourselves. And when we do this, we will show Christ's love in our lives. And by showing Christ in our life, we will have

His strength and His peace. And with that, we will have the joy of the Lord.

> *12 Beloved, do not be surprised at the fiery ordeal among you, which comes upon you for your testing, as though some strange thing were happening to you; 13 but to the degree that you share the sufferings of Christ, keep on rejoicing, so that also at the revelation of His glory you may rejoice with exultation. 1 Peter 4: 12-13*

Chapter 14

Chris: Remember the good and forget the bad.

Chris wanted to focus on the good things that happened to him. He was selected to attend the "Semester at the Sea". This is where students get to literally sail around the world taking college classes on a cruise ship. He was able to hear Fidel Castro give a 3-hour speech. His favorite ports of call were India and Viet Nam. He met many friends and he kept several of these friends for the years following the cruise.

Chris was selected to be a summer intern at Duke University. He also was able to care for children in the university hospital. It was here he confirmed he wanted to become a doctor.

Chris was able to live, work and attend college in a paradise, Hawaii. While in the Army, he was stationed at Schofield Barracks in Hawaii and in Bosnia. He received many military honors. He rose to the rank of Sergeant.

Chris had a family who loved him (and still does). He has a heavenly Father who loves him. He was handsome, slim and athletic. He was smart and had a high GPA in college. He got a high score on his Medical School entrance exams (the MCATs). He was accepted into medical school. We could go on and on. Chris had many people who sincerely cared for him and were devoted to him. Chris had many good things happen to him.

Chris also wanted to forget the bad things that happened to him. Things like an old Jeep that kept breaking down, breakups with girlfriends, strife with parents while he was a teenager in high school, and moving with the family several times when he was growing up. Chris had to live and work through some very difficult challenges.

After he died, countless friends came to us to tell us about Chris. They would tell us Chris would find the good in people others would not choose to acknowledge. This happened even with people he barely came to knew. Chris wanted to encourage anyone he met. He even wanted to encourage those who were not the most popular or pleasant to be around. Chris would reach out to them when others would not.

But through it all, Chris wanted to "*remember the good and forget the bad*". In other words, Chris wanted to forget the bad experiences and remember the positive. He understood even within the bad experiences, positive things could be learned from them. He would say: "In every bad situation something good can come from it".

And what his words mean to us

We should always remember the good things that have happened to us. How we wish we could all live with the attitude of remembering the good and forgetting the bad. Our lives would be much easier if we could accomplish this.

Chris taught us our inner attitudes do not have to conform to the worries, hurts and tragedies that happen in our lives. Chris taught us we have to move beyond these circumstances, forget about them and focus on the good things in our lives. If Chris could do this with all the challenges that happened to him, then we can do it also.

Our life and attitude can be full of joy no matter what happens to us. We need to look at life with the perspective Chris had. In our own lives, we take too seriously unimportant events and circumstances. When this happens, we get discouraged. And when we get discouraged, this attitude can be observed by others.

We can rest assured Jesus Christ is always with us. Someday we will be in heaven with Him and we will have the ultimate joy. But our joy and eternal life can start now. Today our joy should come from knowing Christ is with us and knowing He is in control. Knowing this should make any problems we have seem smaller.

> *4 Rejoice in the Lord always; again I will say, rejoice! 5 Let your gentle spirit be known to all men. The Lord is near. 6 Be anxious for nothing, but in everything by prayer and supplication with thanksgiving let your requests be made known to God. 7 And the peace of God, which surpasses all comprehension, will guard your hearts and your minds in Christ Jesus.   Philippians 4: 4-7*

Chapter 15

Chris: Put the positive people back in your life, no matter what they look like and how they act.

Chris knew the value of keeping positive and encouraging people in his life. He knew it is challenging to look at the bright side of things all on your own. It is always good to have somebody to remind you of the positive things in life. Having positive people come alongside you when you are discouraged can remind you of what you are missing in life.

Chris would surround himself with positive people. He needed these people to show him the positive aspects in life. He had so many wonderful friends. These are friends we did not even know until after he died. These people told us how great and fun loving a person Chris was. How he was positive, refreshing and made people laugh. One look at the many pictures he took with his friends verified this. The pictures were often of funny poses or funny faces he was making in the picture. He was truly having a fun time with his friends.

And what his words mean to us

The important thing is not how people look or how they act, but if they have a positive outlook to life. We each know of these kinds of people who have these kinds of qualities: those who make us laugh, who encourage us, who will be with us no matter what happens. These qualities in people are so much more valuable than appearance or their social status. Good looks will fade, but their positive personalities usually last for a lifetime. And we need these kinds of people when things go bad in our own life. Therefore, we should surround ourselves with people who will encourage us.

Life would be better if we surround ourselves with positive people. People whose attitudes encourage us instead of bringing us down. People who make us laugh instead of people who are constantly depressed. We need people who are optimistic. We need people who give from their hearts, instead of people who are constantly depressed. Yes, these are the kind of people we should have in our lives. The Lord wants us to have close friends who have a joyful outlook on life. Constantly being around critical and negative people can eventually discourage us. The Lord wants us to stay positive, not tear others down or have a negative attitude.

We can control our negative thoughts, no matter what has happened to us. As soon as a negative thought comes into our mind, we need to replace it with a positive thought or talk to a person we know has a positive attitude. We can write positive Life Lessons like Chris did. We will never know how often Chris read his own Life Lessons, but we are sure he did. Even now, we read them over and over and we are encouraged. We just need to keep re-affirming the positive things and blessings in our lives. We need to maintain encouraging thoughts, express optimistic words, and keep constructive people in our lives.

> *31 Let all bitterness and wrath and anger and clamor and slander be put away from you, along with all malice. 32 Be kind to one another, tender-hearted, forgiving each other, just as God in Christ also has forgiven you. Ephesians 4:31-32*

Chapter 16

Chris: Give freely.

C hris was a very generous person. He prided himself on
giving unique gifts. These gifts were thoroughly thought out
and researched ahead of time. You could watch the joy on his face
as he watched you open the gift. Surely one of his talents in life
was giving gifts to others. This fit with everything else about him.

Chris was not a rich person by any means. But Chris would
always find within his means a way to give a special gift to those he
loved. Most often these were not standard gifts. He would look
for the out of the ordinary things to give. He gave his mother a
music box containing photos of him and his sister. Another time
he gave her a small, beautifully decorated metal tree with ornate
leaves. These were gifts often you wanted to have. But often they
were something you would never buy for yourself.

As talented as Chris was in giving gifts, he was weak in
receiving gifts. In his later years, we knew he could use new
clothes or shoes. The clothes he wore at our house were becoming

worn. His favorite shoes were a pair of sneakers that had more holes than Swiss cheese. In addition, these clothes and shoes seemed better suited to the warmer climate in Hawaii, not Chicago. No matter how we begged, he would not let us buy him new clothes.

We never understood the reason he did not like to receive gifts. This was just something about him. He did not want someone to give him a gift. Maybe it was because he thought he should be buying these things for himself or he did not deserve them. Some items he enjoyed receiving were small things he could eat. Things like a special candy bar or beef jerky. When Chris lived in Hawaii and Colorado Springs, Cindy would often send him care packages with these types of articles. But he would not accept anything big or expensive.

One time we learned Chris was having problems with his laptop computer. The problems with the computer were annoyances, but the laptop was still in working order. We decided we would replace the laptop for him. We thought while going to medical school, he was going to need a good, reliable computer. So we went to a local store and bought him another new laptop. Knowing Chris, and just for caution, we left the laptop unopened in the box. Our fear was he would not accept the laptop and we wanted to be able to return it to the store unopened, just in case. As we feared, he would not accept the computer. He could not even give us a reason why he would not accept it. So we disappointedly returned the unopened box to the store. That was just Chris.

The last gift he ever gave his mother was a necklace he bought in Silverton, Colorado. It was a beautiful necklace made of a glass-shaped crystal which had a silhouette of an angel inside. Cindy loved this necklace and of course it was special because it was the last gift she received from him before he died.

Unfortunately, Cindy lost the necklace when the hasp broke. Cindy was heartbroken. Cindy searched frantically for it and we even searched for a replacement on the internet, but to no avail. We telephoned the stores in Silverton where Chris could have purchased the necklace. Again, this was not successful.

One store we contacted recommended we call the Silverton Chamber of Commerce. The person who answered the phone at the Chamber asked Cindy to describe the necklace and she simply promised to do some 'research". The next day we had a message she had found the store that had sold Chris the necklace. She promised to send it to Cindy. When it arrived, there was no listing of the sender's name. Even though we called, she would not leave her name or address so we could send her money for the purchase. Once again, someone like Chris was *giving freely*. And maybe, Chris had a distant hand in this. Maybe he wanted his mother to once again have the last gift he had given her.

And what his words mean to us

Giving freely does not necessarily mean to give material possessions to someone and spend lots of money. *Giving freely* can mean to give your time which is really one of our most valuable possessions. *Giving freely* can be giving away our will to please ourselves and replace it with our willingness to help others. *Giving freely* can mean to replace our ambitions to succeed in this world and replace them with finding ways to serve others. *Giving freely* can mean to give away our freedoms in order to find time to help others. *Giving freely* can be to sacrifice our own comforts, wants and desires for the sake of others. And *giving freely* can mean to give away our rights to our own personal space to allow people to come near us. Chris gave everything he had. He dedicated his life to help others. And like Chris, we should not expect anything in return.

We need to learn to not hang on to or cherish our material possessions. When we are gone from this world, someone will take our earthly things and either put them in boxes, give or throw them away, or hang them in a back part of the closet. After Chris died, we remember so many things of his were given away, thrown away or placed in our closet. We kept several things like letters, photos and military uniforms. These are the things that will maintain our memories. We kept nothing of his which had a material value. There were so few things that had material value.

We need to give out of the goodness of our hearts, knowing Jesus Christ gave up everything He had. He only expected in return our love for Him and turning our lives over to Him. Because God has given us His blessings, we should give generously to others of our time, love and possessions.

Freely you received, freely give. Matthew 10:8b

Chapter 17

Chris: Try to live positively and let nothing get you down.

Chris tried to focus on the positive side of life and worked hard never to be negative. He did not want to let his personal problems get him down when he was in the presence of others. The last thing he wanted to do was to drag others down with negativity. Chris often worried about taking his medical school entrance exam. So when he needed to be alone and study, he would leave his friends with a smile and a joke and then close himself in his room and pour himself into his books.

Among his friends Chris wanted to encourage others. His friends told us how people were naturally attracted to Chris because of his positive energy. When he was with his friends, there never seemed to be a dull moment. Chris had a fun-loving nature and he was happy around his friends. This is the way he wanted to live his life. He wanted to have a joyful time and he wanted others to be happy and to have fun. If you look at his pictures with his friends, Chris was often the "goofy" one in the photo doing a silly pose.

People also valued Chris's presence when he was around them. Chris was a pleasant person to be around. We all know these kinds of people. The kind of person who is always happy and smiling. These kinds of people have a positive vibration coming from them and they simply make you feel better. When you are around such people, life seems to be a less stressful, you are more open to others and you feel less intimidated. Life for a period of time seems to be less serious and it is easier to laugh and enjoy yourself and others.

And what his words mean to us

A story in Nehemiah 4: 11-14 describes how the Jews rebuilding the wall became tired and worn out. Enemies were using threats to discourage them. The Jews wanted to give up even though they had completed one half the wall in only 26 days. Nehemiah told them in verse 14: *When I saw their fear, I rose and spoke to the nobles, the officials and the rest of the people : "Do not be afraid of them; remember the Lord who is great and awesome, and fight for your brothers, your sons, your daughters, your wives and your houses.".*

The way to fight fatigue and the daunting tasks ahead of us is to focus on the Lord. We need to adapt and adjust to the issues causing our discouragement. Instead of just sitting back and continuing to be discouraged, we can change what we are doing and get our focus back on God. One way to have a positive attitude is to do what Nehemiah did in chapter 4:16. He fought the discouragement in the people by changing how the Jews were building the wall. He added security men to make everyone feel more reassured of their safety. He directed his people to stick together. Nehemiah illustrated how a leader was going to lead by working right alongside the people. He wanted them to take up the challenge before them. And like Chris did with his friends, we can set the example for others.

Psalm 84:5-7 describes how we get our strength from the Lord as we search for Him. As we go on our life journey we will be walking through the Valley of Baca, which is translated as a "valley of weeping". Walking through the valley could be a symbol of the struggles and tears we walk through to find God. We all have barren places in our life and we all have struggles. We find we can make this barren valley *"a spring"* and allow *"The early rain also covers it with blessings"*. We need to remember the culmination of our journey is to appear before God. Therefore, we should focus on the end of the journey and not on the struggles and trials along the way.

When we get discouraged, we need to look up and remember God is in control. He has a good and perfect plan for our life. We need to focus on all the blessings we have. God would not have allowed something bad to happen in our life unless something good was going to come from it. Said in another way, when something bad is happening in our life, it is not happening to us, but it is happening for us. Even with all the bad things that happened to Chris, he tried not to have a victim mentality. Therefore, he taught us to *"try to live positively and let nothing get you down."*

> **5** *How blessed is the man whose strength is in You, In whose heart are the highways to Zion!* **6** *Passing through the valley of Baca they make it a spring ; The early rain also covers it with blessings.* **7** *They go from strength to strength, Every one of them appears before God in Zion. Psalm 84:5-7*

Chapter 18

Chris: Volunteer and give freely.

Whether rich or poor we all have the same valuable asset: our time. Chris never had a lot of money, so he gave freely of his time. He volunteered to many causes and expected nothing in return. He found it rewarding to help and encourage people. Chris wanted to set the example to others to *give freely*. Chris wanted to leave his legacy as someone who helped others in need, with no strings attached. In this way, he demonstrated a giving heart. He showed us generosity while still having a small bank account.

Chris volunteered in many ways. He organized a car wash and donated the money to orphans at Premananda Orphan Center in India. He helped others students with their homework. He organized a recycling program at Chaminade. He volunteered for extra duties in the Army, even though he knew there was no extra reward. He gave rides to friends who did not have cars.

Chris taught himself how to cook. Since he did not have extra cash for dining at top-end restaurants, he cooked gourmet meals for his friends and family. One of the greatest gifts he ever gave his mother was on her birthday in 2010. It was a gourmet meal which included lobster and bananas foster. This was only three weeks before he went home to be with the Lord.

Chris also prided himself as a guide to friends on adventurous hiking trips. Hiking does not require any money and it was a great entertainment he could provide to others. Chris loved to lead others into the dense forests in Hawaii or into the backcountry of Colorado. He knew where to find the remote waterfall or the panoramic vista you could only see by getting out of your car and setting off on foot. More than enjoying the hike itself, he enjoyed giving others the fascination and majesty of the outdoors. And of course, he would never give up until he reached the place he wanted to go. This meant he would exhort others to finish the journey to make it to the top of the mountain or to see the beauty of the waterfall.

And what his words mean to us

A former church gave us a t-shirt which provides a definition of generosity. It is "freedom from smallness of heart". This sums it up. The world tells us to save and keep everything we can. We desire a big bank account and we keep our garages and storage bins full of things we "may" need someday. But God blesses those who give freely of their money and possessions and he blesses those who have a big heart. We have found when we give freely, God blesses us with more so we can increase our generosity.

A giving heart also puts our possessions into the right perspective. Even though Chris did not have a lot of possessions, after he died we boxed up many things and gave them away. Someday, someone will give our possessions away also. If we are generous in the way God wants us to be, we will realize our possessions do not belong to us in the first place. They are given to us by God to help others. If we are generous with our possessions, we are not their captive. We are free to help others. This is how our Lord wants us to be.

The same can be said for our time, which is actually another of our possessions. What better way to spend our time than to help others and encourage them. We need to free ourselves from things that rob us of our time where we not available to help and encourage others. Many of us do not have a wealth of money, but all of us have the same amount of time to bless others. We just need to find the ways to do it.

> *18 Instruct them to do good, to be rich in good works, to be generous and ready to share, 19 storing up for themselves the treasure of a good foundation for the future, so that they may take hold of that which is life indeed. I Timothy 6:18-19*

Chapter 19

Chris: Take care of God's creatures.

Chris had a deep appreciation for all of God's creations. He especially enjoyed the fish in the ocean. When Chris visited Africa, he told us stories of how he was amazed by the freedom of the creatures running free in the wilderness. He advocated for causes to keep the ocean and forests clean and healthy. We cannot recall a time when Chris went hunting. Lindsey remembers how Chris would not even kill insects inside the home. He would simply catch them and take them outside.

Later in his life, Chris stopped visiting zoological gardens because he simply saw wild animals being kept captive. One summer we took the family to a zoo in Colorado Springs. They only thing we can now remember about this day is Chris hated the entire walk! He was especially sad when he saw the bald eagle, his favorite bird, inside a small cage. We believe if he had found the key to the gate, he would have released it. *And what his words mean to us*

Psalm 148 gives a beautiful description of how all of God's creations, including animals, were made with the power and ability to glorify our Lord. In this way, we as human beings share in our praise and worship with all God's creatures.

It is not God's intention that we place animals above human life. God wanted to bless mankind with a wonderful world he created for us. He placed animals here for our enjoyment. We are responsible to treat and care for these animals the same way He cares for us.

> *7 Praise the LORD from the earth, Sea monsters and all deeps; **10** Beasts and all cattle; Creeping things and winged fowl; **13** Let them praise the name of the LORD, For His name alone is exalted; His glory is above earth and heaven. Psalm 148: 7, 10, 13*

Value of Persistence and Commitment

Chapter 20

Chris: Seeking something that seems impossible must take persistence and the desire to not give up even if it seems incredibly foolish and is.

Chris never did anything half-heartedly. Whatever he set out to do, he wanted to excel at it. He did this at a young age with soccer and later in life with rock climbing. He believed you could have anything in life as long as you were patient and gave all your effort to succeed.

Chris's dream was to be a doctor in a third world country to help the people who could not care for themselves. To Chris, and many others, it seemed impossible in many ways. It seemed impossible to be able to get the funds to go to school, to get a high enough score on his medical school entrance exams (MCAT) and get accepted into medical school. But Chris was a fighter. He dreamed his dream and he worked tirelessly for it.

To Chris, this dream of going to medical school seemed impossible. But he never gave up. He believed he needed to continue to try, even though it seemed foolish. He wanted to keep trying and keep moving forward.

Chris continued to show his persistence to pursue his dream. To help pay his bills, Chris worked odd, low-paying jobs and jobs no one else would want to do. While in Colorado Springs studying for his MCAT exams, Chris took care of an older gentleman with Multiple Sclerosis. Chris told us stories about how this man was not the most pleasant person to be around. He was understandably cranky and unappreciative of those who cared for him. But Chris did this because it afforded him the hours and schedule he needed to study for his MCAT exams.

It was hard to explain what drove him so hard to become a doctor. It certainly was a hard path to take. And it was certainly not for the money since he wanted to be a doctor in a third world country. We guess it was his desire to achieve his dream to help others who could not afford to care for themselves. He was told by several he could take an easier road. He could do something easier than going to medical school and becoming a doctor. Some thought he was foolish to work so hard, study so hard, and pursue a dream which would take 6 years to achieve once he got into medical school.

With this Life Lesson, maybe even Chris thought it was foolish. He added the last phrase: "*incredibility foolish and is*". But becoming a doctor was his dream. No matter what "cards he was dealt", he demonstrated he was not going to give up. He was going to succeed. And enough people surrounded him to keep him moving towards his dream.

And what his words mean to us

We have never experienced the same types of hardships and sufferings Chris did. Hopefully, we never will. But one thing we have learned: persevering through these types of hardships and difficulties produces a stronger character in us. No one likes the pain and suffering that goes along with hardships and difficulties. But what we have learned is with all the pain we have gone through since Chris died, it has made us stronger. We have a desire to help others who are hurting. We now desire to come alongside someone who has lost a loved one, help the person on the street who is hungry or help the poor and destitute in a third world country to find a clean source of water to drink. Character is the way we show to others what we are made of and how we cope with the difficult times.

Going through difficult times has also strengthened our faith in God. We have greater confidence and certainty in the future knowing God is in control. We know we will never understand God, but we know he has a will and plan for our lives, just like He had a will and plan for Chris's life.

Since Chris died, one of our favorite poems is one written by Dora Greenwell. She wrote this poem in the 1800's. Aaron Shust used this poem for much of his lyrics to a modern-day song called "My Savior My God". The words that comfort us the most are the first four lines of the poem:

> *I am not skilled to understand*
> *What God has willed, what God has planned*
> *I only know at His right hand*
> *Stands one who is my Savior*

We now feel comfortable we will not fully understand why Chris left us at the young age of 30. Suffice to say we are convinced no one here on earth will fully understand God. But like the poem says, we are convinced He is my Savior. Because of this, we can know about Jesus and commune with Him. And best of all, someday we will live with Jesus in heaven. Chris is already experiencing this.

> *1 Therefore, having been justified by faith, we have peace with God through our Lord Jesus Christ, 2 through whom also we have obtained our introduction by faith into this grace in which we stand; and we exult in hope of the glory of God. 3 And not only this, but we also exult in our tribulations, knowing that tribulation brings about perseverance; 4 and perseverance, proven character; and proven character, hope; 5 and hope does not disappoint, because the love of God has been poured out within our hearts through the Holy Spirit who was given to us. Romans 5: 1-5*

Chapter 21

Chris: When in the work environment, try to be diligent and love what you do.

Chris was always humble in his work environment. He told us at his internship at Duke University he loved to work with children with special needs in the university hospital. While he lived in Colorado Springs, Colorado, he took care of a paraplegic as part-time employment while he was studying for his medical school entrance exams. He would say he never wanted to go into his work with a bad attitude. Even on the days that were going badly for Chris, he did not want to let it affect him and show other people how it affected him.

One summer in college he worked as a missionary at Intervarsity Christian Family Camp in Colorado Springs, Colorado. This family camp was very much like a dude ranch, only it included Christian education and children's programs.

The college students taught the children, or they would have duties such as taking care of the horses, cooking or general maintenance. Chris was assigned some of the hardest jobs while at the camp. But he loved being there.

One of the highlights for the camp guests was the Wrangler's Breakfast. It was served at sunrise on the mountain above the camp. Chris would get up before sunrise, load the food into the truck and drive up the road to start the campfire and set up the tables. He would do this five days a week. After cooking breakfast, he would then do other things such as digging post holes and repairing fences. Chris remained diligent and loved serving the Lord and the family campers.

Chris usually desired a line of work serving someone else. We want to believe deep down Chris believed he was not working for man, but for the Lord. Even though on some days it was frustrating and very hard work, Chris knew he was working for a higher purpose. Every time we looked, it seemed Chris was either working with a special needs child, a paraplegic, or studying to become a doctor in a third world country. Chris realized he was going to face unpleasant and hard times in the work place, but he also recognized he had to keep going and not get discouraged.

Chris remained diligent in pursuing his dream of being a doctor in a third world country. Some of us can only aspire to our dream job. Chris continued with a constant effort to accomplish what he felt he was called to do. He would study for long hours to prepare for his medical school entrance exams (MCATs). When studying for his classes while in medical school, we saw him take a 10 minute break, take a deep breath and then go right back to studying again. Even though these jobs and medical school were extremely hard, he remained devoted and loved what he was doing.

Chris loved whatever job he had. No matter if he was digging holes for fence posts in the hard soil in the mountains, digging trenches for a foundation for a church at a mission in Laredo, Mexico or taking care of a paraplegic in Colorado while studying for medical school entrance exams. No matter what job he had, he remembered it was a gift from the Lord.

And what his words mean to us

We need to love whatever we are doing and love the chance we get to do it. Even though the current work we are doing may not be our dream job, the Lord has blessed us to serve Him. So many these days of this writing are unemployed or underemployed. Realizing this makes us thankful for any job the Lord has given us. We can be so much happier if we keep a great attitude and love what we do, no matter the circumstances.

We also need to be diligent in what we do. We should not just 'put in the time' in the job we do, but we also need to be diligent at it. To be diligent means to be earnest and steady, even painstaking. We need to do this in any job we have. Whether it is at the job we have at a company, or working with toddlers on Sunday morning in church. If we are diligent at the job we have and love our job, we will refrain from complaining. We will show others at work a great attitude. We will also show those we work for we are an employee with the behaviors they want others to emulate. If we do this, we do not need to be the smartest employee at work. We will be successful if we demonstrate a good attitude, diligence in what we are doing and a love and appreciation for our job.

> **12** *I know that there is nothing better for them*
> *than to rejoice and to do good in one's lifetime;*
> **13** *moreover, that every man who eats and drinks*
> *sees good in all his labor -it is the gift of God.*
> *Ecclesiastes 3:12-13*

Chapter 22

Chris: Don't make excuses for why someone else is successful and you are not.

Chris was bright, handsome and had many friends. But Chris had some difficult challenges in life. Some of these challenges took him into despair and into valleys. At times, he felt cheated in life and did not understand why so many bad things had happened to him.

It would have been easy for Chris to make excuses for why bad things happened to him. It would have been easy for him to give up. In this Life Lesson, Chris reminded himself not to make excuses why others seemingly had an easier road in life than he did. He saw others were obtaining their goals in life at a much younger age. He felt he had to work evener harder than his peers to accomplish the same things. He believed he had to put forth more effort to overcome the challenges that came along, while others had an easier path.

Even with the long and difficult roads Chris had to travel, he did not make excuses. He knew if he started making excuses, it was the prelude of giving up on his dream. He could have compared himself to others and become depressed. He could have fallen into self-pity and concluded life was just not fair to him. But giving up was the last thing Chris wanted to do.

So Chris persevered. He looked at a new valley in his life as one he had to march through. Each challenge that came along in his life was like another obstacle he had to overcome. He so wanted to achieve his dream of becoming a doctor in a third-world country, he worked tirelessly and did not make excuses.

And what his words mean to us

We need to examine our own life's journeys: both the good times and the bad. When the trials come, how do we handle them? Do we make excuses? Do we blame others? Do we hold grudges? After Chris died, I forgave someone who deeply hurt me. I blamed this person for the heartaches in my life. Now, I have let the hurts go just like Chris let go of his bad memories. Chris and I were both better persons for having done so.

An important question for this Life Lesson is: "how do we describe success"? If you believe *"someone else is successful, and you are not",* what does this kind of success look like? Is success having a senior-level position at work, a big bank account, a large house in a nice part of town and a nice car? This may be how the world defines success, but this is not how the Lord defines it. We can attest these things do not guarantee happiness in life. In fact, these possessions can have the opposite effect. Having a nice, big home can be an anchor around your neck if you need to sell the home. Having a nice, expensive car can be costly when it comes to insuring or repairing the car. Having a senior-level position at work can be very strenuous with all the back-biting and politics often associated at those jobs.

My personal hero while growing up was my father: Edward Warren Dunlap. My father and mother did not have a lot of money, a fancy car or a large home. They lived in a small town and worked on their small farm. They were happy and they had what they needed in life. I was also happy growing up in their home. My mother and father sent all three children to college. From my perspective, they were successful in life. Therefore, success is not defined by the amount of possessions we have.

When we make excuses in our lives, we often do not want to face up to our own shortcomings. It seems easier to just blame others. Or it is easier to refuse to believe or accept what others are saying to us. It may actually be good, constructive criticism we need to hear. Unfortunately, it is so much easier just to blame others and not look in the mirror. Therefore, we need to humble ourselves, choose the high road and not make excuses.

> *17 for the kingdom of God is not eating and drinking, but righteousness and peace and joy in the Holy Spirit. 18 For he who in this way serves Christ is acceptable to God and approved by men. 19 So then we pursue the things which make for peace and the building up of one another. Romans 14:17-19*

Chapter 23

Chris: Ask for advice on what the appropriate situation is. Try to select the most level-headed person to ask this.

While most of us value our own opinions based on the belief our views and judgments are superior to others, Chris often sought advice from others. Chris used this Life Lesson many times while he was in the Army and in school. As level-headed as Chris was, he knew he needed to seek advice from others. He valued the wisdom and counsel he received from the people he respected the most. Chris would swallow his ego and seek the counsel of those he had recognized with integrity. Many men have such egos we do not even ask for directions. Chris trusted the thoughts of those who had walked his journey before him. He wanted to keep an open mind to learn the wisdom of others who had already lived through the trials where he wanted to go. Some of the people he sought advice from were older such as Army Officers and professors at Chaminade, University of Hawaii and the Chicago College of Medicine. If he wanted advice on relationships, he would ask his trusted friends. After he sought the advice from others, he would always correctly put the ultimate trust in himself.

And what his words mean to us

For those of us who are older, seeking advice from those more knowledgeable is awkward. We were taught in school to be individuals, do our own homework and do our own projects. We learned to question ourselves if we needed to ask advice from others. Will we be imposing? Will we appear lazy? Will we appear incompetent? Will we ask a foolish question?

We should not have inhibitions about seeking advice. In Proverbs we are encouraged to seek out wise men and listen to their counsel. At the workplace today it is essential to use teamwork to harness the abilities, knowledge and wisdom of everyone on the team. This enhances and improves the final result. If we only listen to ourselves and we only value our own wisdom, we are in bad company. Proverbs would label us "foolish" not to seek advice from others.

The way of a fool is right in his own eyes, But a wise man is he who listens to counsel. Proverbs 12:15

Chapter 24

Chris: In the classroom, don't stand out until you have a good feel for what is appropriate. Also, don't be a know-it-all at any point in time, ever. The quiet people don't like it.

Chris was often the class clown. But wisely he realized there was an appropriate time and place for standing out in a classroom. Chris was careful not to be overbearing to others in the class who were quieter, shy or who mostly kept their thoughts and feelings to themselves. Chris would make note of those who were more introverted in a class and then tone down his outgoing nature. This is because Chris wanted to be careful to respect the rights of others and not offend or intimidate those who were quieter. He certainly did not want to come across to the class as someone who thought he knew everything and refused to listen to others. His nature was to include everyone, especially if their personalities, feelings and personal characteristics were different from his.

Chris would quickly volunteer for anything and everything. He always wanted to participate in or lead whatever project was going on at the time. Realizing this was his nature, he would also be conscious to gauge the class surroundings and give the quieter classmates an opportunity to step up.

<u>And what his words mean to us</u>

We should be conscious of our own personal characteristics of how we interact with others. We should strive to demonstrate the characteristics of Christ and the love of God. We should have unity with others and make an effort to include everyone. We should be sympathetic and considerate to the needs of those who come across our path. We should demonstrate brotherly love. We should have a tender heart and be sensitive to the needs of those who are different. We need to exhibit humility and think less of our own needs and more of the needs of those around us. We need to be willing to include and encourage everyone and rejoice when they participate.

> *To sum up, all of you be harmonious,*
> *sympathetic, brotherly, kindhearted, and humble*
> *in spirit; I Peter 3:8*

Why Faith is Indispensable

Chapter 25

Chris: Waiting often hurts a lot and leaves you lost in the woods. I have no idea what to expect tomorrow, next week, next month, but I still have faith.

Chris often had to experience waiting in his young life. Chris made a terrible mistake in judgment at Chaminade University in Honolulu, Hawaii. No apology or offer of restitution to Chaminade University could save him. He was dismissed three days before graduation. Flight plans by the family to see him graduate were canceled. He was totally devastated and morally broken to his very core.

This haunted him for the rest of his young life. He was severely depressed and embarrassed. He removed himself from contact from all his family and most of his closest friends. He finished his undergraduate degree at the University of Hawaii. Even though a tragedy, this was likely the start of Chris's deep faith in Jesus Christ.

So Chris knew the meaning of waiting and being lost. He did not know if his dream of becoming a doctor could ever become true. Becoming a doctor was what he cared about most. He cared more about being a doctor than he cared for friends, family and even his closest girlfriends. This desire is what drove him.

After the incident, he did not know what to expect. Was all his hard work in school lost? Should he keep trying to graduate by enrolling in the University of Hawaii? Was it worth taking off an entire year to study for the Medical School entrance exams (called MCATs), or was it a waste of time? He was humbled as he had never been in life.

Chris was waiting for what path God wanted for him. But waiting was hard for Chris. He always struggled with patience. Chris often wanted to know things immediately. Chris was conscious of his age in medical school. Therefore he wanted to have things happen quickly. He wanted to know God's plan for his life. He wanted to know his purpose.

Chris knew somehow God was going to get him into medical school. He knew he would never succeed on his own; God would have to do it. Therefore Chris trusted that God was in control. He just had to be patient and wait upon the Lord.

But one thing about Chris was he did not give up. He still had faith. He had faith something good was going to happen to him. He did not know what it was, but he was going to trust the Lord was going to make something good happen.

And what his words mean to us

Waiting is often painful and leaves one wondering if God is out there. Is He listening and watching? Do we feel His presence? Does God even care? We need to remember the Lord is always there. We need to trust Him, even though we sometimes do not feel His presence. Even when all seems lost, we should never give up. We should always have faith the Lord has a plan for us. We may not know what the plan is, but we need to have faith He is always watching over us and has a plan for our lives.

Chris's Life Lesson reminds us waiting is part of God's plan. Like Chris, we have no idea what to expect in the future. And like this Life Lesson, we need to have faith He will show us what His plan is for our lives. We need to hope and put our trust in Him. But at the same time, we need to be diligent to look for opportunities to serve Him. We cannot sit around and just wait to let the Lord whisper something in our ears. Growing up on a small farm, I realized we needed to plow the fields and plant seeds before a harvest would come. In the same way, we need to be diligent in looking for opportunities to serve the Lord and preparing to serve Him. Then we can be patient and wait for Him to fulfill His promises. This is exactly what Chris did.

The word "wait" infers the sense of expecting. We need to wait on God and have a sense of expecting from Him. Isaiah 40:31 refers to those who were suffering a long and terrible captivity in Babylon. So it applies to those who were feeling weak, guilty and helpless. The verse says to put their trust in the Lord and wait for His help. We also should never give up and we should continue in our faith. Life will never be easy. It seemed like life was especially hard for Chris, but he *"still had faith"*.

> *Yet those who wait for the LORD will gain new strength ; They will mount up with wings like eagles, They will run and not get tired, They will walk and not become weary. Isaiah 40:31*

Chapter 26

Chris: Have faith that this is what God wants for you; especially when you are lonely.

C hris had a lot of challenges and trials to test his faith. While in college and after college, he often wondered why so many bad things happened to him. Time after time, obstacles would come up to block his path and his dreams. He knew God had a plan for him, he just did not know what it was. He often would journey and struggle through these challenges alone, not telling anyone the struggles he was facing in his mind. Even with all the friends he had, and with all those who loved him dearly, Chris experienced loneliness and this brought him down. He felt he must 'climb the mountain' of becoming a doctor alone. There is no deeper sadness than feeling you are facing the challenges of this world totally alone.

Chris remained faithful. Chris asked God for guidance because he knew God was leading him somewhere. He wanted God's direction in his life so he often wondered and asked God why the path was so hard. He saw others having an easier life, but others were not climbing the same high mountain he was.

In his entire life, Chis was never content to take the easy road. If the task was easy, Chris seemed bored and unchallenged with it. He pushed himself to the brink, never being satisfied with mediocrity. He also pushed and encouraged others to make themselves everything they could be. If someone was struggling, Chris would come alongside them to encourage them. He did not want others to feel the loneliness he was feeling inside.

And what his words mean to us

In Psalm 25, David was lonely and afflicted and he asked God for guidance. The Psalm shows David had reached a point when he was so discouraged he earnestly sought after God and was desperately seeking to be taught by God. To be taught by God, we must seek Him in prayer and read His Word. Then once we receive His guidance, we must obey.

We know we must remain faithful in whatever plan the Lord has for us. Even though we do not know what it is, we know His plan is out there and He is watching over us. As Psalm 25 says, we need to ask Him to show us His ways. We need to trust in Him. We need to let Him lead us in His plan.

We should not ask God to bless "my" plan for "my" life. So often we do that. We want to be the captain and ask God to bless "my" plans. We ask God to bless the things we want or to answer the prayers for what we want. Even though David was a King, he wanted the Lord to teach him His ways and His paths. David put his hope in the Lord "all day long".

We found it fascinating in verse 16 David said "*I am lonely and afflicted*". Chris's Life Lesson also said "*especially when you are lonely*". We need to understand, like Chris did, sometimes we will go through lonely times in our lives. Especially during those times, all of us need to realize, more than ever, the Lord will guide us and direct us through the valley and the dark times in our life. Psalm 23:4 says "*Even though I walk through the valley of the shadow of death*". The point is we do walk "through the valley". This implies we will always emerge out the other side of the valley; we will not stay in it. And we will always come out the other side of the valley if we trust Him and let Him lead us.

As you are reading this book, you may be experiencing a downward spiral and you may feel lonely. God is the only one who can lift you out of your pain. God can lift you out of your loneliness. God can turn our challenges and our problems into victories, but the victories may not come right away. Seek Him. Cry out to God like David did. When you are willing to do that, God is always there waiting for you.

> *4 Make me know Your ways, O LORD ; Teach me Your paths. 5 Lead me in Your truth and teach me, For You are the God of my salvation ; For You I wait all the day. 16 Turn to me and be gracious to me, For I am lonely and afflicted.*
> *Psalm 25: 4-5, 16*

Chapter 27

Chris: Go to church and breathe deeply.

Chris believed it was important to go to church to worship God. We could tell he made going to church a priority in his life. Even though he did not talk much about his faith to his family, many of his friends told us how he shared his faith with them. Even though the time he spent on his medical school studies was enormous and it occupied almost every waking moment, Chris would find time to go to a local church on Sunday morning.

He always went to a church he selected personally. When we asked him to go to church with us, he always wanted to go to a local Episcopal Church and worship there. We think it was something to do with the quiet worship and singing of hymns which attracted him to the Episcopal Church.

Chris also included the "*breathe deeply*" when he wrote "*go to church*". He shared often he felt the Lord was guiding him and was watching after him. We believe Chris wanted to *"breathe in his Word"* and meditate on His Word. When Chris went to church, it helped him reflect on what was really important in life. It helped him focus on the Lord and His work, and not on the problems in life. Church was a place that brought Chris comfort and peace. At church, Chris was able to *"breathe deeply"*, release his worries and reflect on what the Lord was saying to him. Chris believed on a Sunday morning, you could give the Lord all your worries and stresses. Sunday was the one day of the week when Chris could go to church and release all the stress and pressure from the other six days of the week. Chris could release them to the Lord.

God's house was a refuge for Chris. Chris could go there and receive the comfort from the Holy Spirit and the Lord. He could step into the Lord's house, relax and feel God's love. This was rewarding to Chris. Chris would *"breathe deeply"* and focus on Christ. Chris knew the Lord loved him unconditionally.

Chris believed he was admitted into medical school only by God demonstrating His grace. Chris had no tattoos, which is a minor miracle in itself after 4 years in the US Army. But he spoke of putting a tattoo of four simple letters on his wrist under his watchband. The four letters would represent four words. We not recall the exact words. We wish we did. We do remember it was four words recognizing God had guided him and blessed him. He never wanted to forget God's grace. Going to church allowed him to breathe deeply and recognize God's presence in his life. In turn, he wanted to bless others the way God had blessed him.

And what his words mean to us

We can commune with God in church. It is so special to us he ended this Life Lesson with *"and breathe deeply"*. To us, this was like taking in a big deep breath where Chris let the love of the Holy Spirit completely immerse him. We need to experience this also. Many of us go to church with the hope of listening to a good sermon, singing a few songs and meeting with our friends. Chris went to church to let the Lord bless him and then for Chris to bless the Lord. At church Chris was experiencing God in such ways we not often do. For Chris it was all about experiencing and "drinking in" the love, joy and peace gained from a Father - child relationship. It was the relationship between him and God. We think Chris loved God with all his heart, soul and mind. While we often experience church as an event to attend once a week, Chris experienced church as a refuge. Chris would go to meditate and worship God.

God manifests his love to us like the feelings and love of a parent. He treats us with tenderness like a mother would for her children. Likewise, God tenderly provides for the church. He gives us peace like a river and He promises to prosper us. Maybe He will not prosper us with money or wealth, but Chris knew God prospers us in many ways. God gave Chris a peace. Like Chris, we just have to accept the peace only He can give.

We need to breathe deeply and pull in the love and comfort of God. We need to let God into our lives and let Him show us how to have peace. God gives to us out of His abundance. He will never leave us or fail us. Although we can choose to walk away from His love, His love always remains.

Imagine a gentle waterfall where you are standing in the falling water. The falling water represents God's love for us. It is gentle and cool. We can choose to walk away from the waterfall, even though the waterfall remains. When we walk away, we miss the gentle water and cool feelings. When we walk away, it is not God who stopped loving us. The waterfall is still there. We just walked away from it. However, like the prodigal son in Luke 11, we can walk back into the water to once again experience His great love.

> *Peace I leave with you; My peace I give to you; not as the world gives do I give to you. Do not let your heart be troubled, nor let it be fearful. John 14:27*

Chapter 28

Chris: Believe in God. Although his plan may seem impossible, it is still a plan.

Chris remained faithful in believing God had a plan for his life. Even with all the challenges he experienced, Chris believed God had a plan for him and God would see this plan through.

Chris was not sure how God was going to get him into medical school, but he certainly believed God had a plan to accomplish it. It seemed Chris was constantly studying for his medical school entrance exams. He studied his undergraduate chemistry books, biology books and anatomy books most every waking hour. Chris worked part-time jobs and lived with little income so he could spend more time studying.

One cold and dark evening in Colorado, I was leaving a restaurant after eating a nice dinner with my sister. She lives in

Greeley, Colorado and we see each other only about twice each year. Chris had tried to call me, but my mobile phone must have been outside of coverage. As my sister and I were standing in the parking lot ready to leave in our separate vehicles, Chris reached my sister on her mobile phone. He called her to let me know he had been accepted into a medical school in Denver. I wept. I was not sure I believed it would ever happen. But Chris never stopped believing God had a plan. That was one of the major differences between him and me. I had my doubts, but Chris believed nothing was impossible for God and God's plans would be carried out. Chris knew he just had to keep believing and studying. Chris knew God was always with him. Chris knew God would accomplish His design for him. He knew it was a good plan. Chris did not know or understand what God's plan was, but he remained faithful God was going to accomplish it, even though it *"seemed impossible"*.

Chris left his destiny in God's hands. God's plan seemed impossible to many, but it never seemed impossible to Chris. Chris knew he could not accomplish getting into medical school on his own merits. He let the Lord "take the steering wheel" of his life and he let the Lord sit in the driver's seat. He let the Lord take control of his future. Chris would simply continue to humble himself and seek and trust in God's direction.

And what his words mean to us

We need to continue in faith, no matter the circumstances. In Matthew 9: 27-31, two blind men followed Jesus and called out to Him for mercy. Jesus did not heal the blind men on the spot, but He let them continue to follow Him after he had gone indoors. Jesus then asked the blind men, "Do you believe I am able to do this?" When they replied yes, Jesus said *"It shall be done to you according to your faith"*. The blind men were then able to see. Jesus wanted to understand and even asked them directly if they really believed He could heal them. Jesus wanted to see if they had faith.

We sometimes think God is not listening to our prayers. We also think God is sometimes too slow in answering our prayers. God may be testing us to make sure we will continue in our faith. We believe Chris lived out his faith in the Lord by never giving up on believing God had a plan. Chris demonstrated he believed God had a plan even though it "*seemed impossible*". Chris wanted God's help in getting into medical school, as much as the blind men wanted to see. The blind men followed Jesus until they received what they wanted. Likewise, Chris continued to pray and study for five years until the Lord allowed him to be accepted into medical school. The men overcame blindness. Chris never gave up in believing. We need to remember to never give up also in believing God has a plan for our lives.

> *By Dorothy Greenwell in 1873*
> *I am not skilled to understand*
> *What God hath willed, what God hath planned;*
> *I only know that at His right hand*
> *Is One Who is my Savior!*
>
> *I take Him at His word indeed;*
> *"Christ died for sinners"—this I read;*
> *For in my heart I find a need*
> *Of Him to be my Savior!*
>
> *That He should leave His place on high*
> *And come for sinful man to die,*
> *You count it strange? So once did I,*
> *Before I knew my Savior!*
>
> *And oh, that He fulfilled may see*
> *The travail of His soul in me,*

And with His work contented be,
As I with my dear Savior!

Yea, living, dying, let me bring
My strength, my solace from this Spring;
That He Who lives to be my King
Once died to be my Savior!

Chapter 29

Chris: Today you've had your greatest accomplishment, thanks to the mercy of the Lord.

In 2010 Chris was accepted into two different medical schools. One medical school was in Colorado and one in Illinois. He selected the medical school in Downers Grove, Illinois and decided to live at home.

Chris worked very hard to get a high grade point average in undergraduate school and a high score on his medical school entrance exams. He knew his acceptance into medical school was his *greatest accomplishment*. He had studied endlessly for nearly 10 years. He had done it the hard way by putting himself through undergraduate school.

When Chris learned of his *greatest accomplishment,* he wrote he gave *thanks to the mercy of the Lord*. Chris remembered the Lord had promised to never forsake him or turn away from him. The Lord carried him through all his struggles, trials and heartaches he endured. Even in the silence of his room where he likely wrote this Life Lesson to himself, Chris did not show pride in his own endurance, intelligence, or merits. Rather, Chris gave credit to the Lord for His mercy and grace he freely gave to him throughout his life.

<u>And what his words mean to us</u>

Cindy and I sometimes think we have made great accomplishments. This leads to pride. We need to reflect back in our lives and see the mercy of God. We can see how He carried us through the difficult times. He showed us mercy in all the different jobs we had and He protected us by not giving us some of the jobs we wanted. The Lord protected us in all the different places we have lived. The Lord has reminded us we can only boast in our knowledge and trust of Him, and not in our accomplishments. It is humbling to us how God chose to show us grace as we walked through this earth. What did we do to deserve it? The answer is simple: we did very little. We simply trusted the Lord has a plan for our lives and we can feel confident in His plan.

God loves us so much. He gives us a joy and a hope through Jesus Christ. By His grace, He lavishes upon us what we do not deserve or earn. He promises us an inheritance in heaven that will never perish, spoil or fade away. We also realize our hope does not only lie with things that will be given to us once we reach heaven. Our hope exists now because he is carrying us through the trials we face while here on earth.

> *3 Blessed be the God and Father of our Lord*
> *Jesus Christ, who according to His great mercy*
> *has caused us to be born again to a living hope*
> *through the resurrection of Jesus Christ from*
> *the dead, 4 to obtain an inheritance which is*
> *imperishable and undefiled and will not fade*

*away, reserved in heaven for you, 5 who are
protected by the power of God through faith for
a salvation ready to be revealed in the last time.
I Peter 1: 3-5*

Managing Relationships While Managing Yourself

Chapter 30

Chris: You never know how much some people care about you until you are heading away so cherish every moment.

After Chris died, the family was astounded by the outpouring of love expressed to us by his friends. He had friends we never knew he had. These were friends who lived all over the world. Friends he met while in the Army and in college.

He likely did not know how much he was loved by his friends and family. His friends wrote letters to us, called us and posted messages on his Facebook® site. They told us how much Chris meant to them, how he had inspired them and how Chris had encouraged them. We received letters from people who expressed such love for him. Truly Chris had touched many people and so many people looked up to him. We will never know if he knew the lasting influence he had on his friends.

His friends told us countless stories of how kind and caring a person Chris was. After high school, Chris was either serving in the Army or a college student. Therefore, Chris never did have a lot of money. So he was always taking his friends to activities that did not cost a lot of money. Activities like mountain hikes, surfing, rock climbing, kayaking to small, remote islands off the coast of Hawaii and just hanging out at the beach. They told us how much fun Chris was and how he was always doing funny things and leading people to get out of their 'shell' and enjoy the life they had.

At one point in college, we now know Chris was depressed and headed away from his friends. We suspect this was the time his friends rallied around him and tried to encourage him. This was also likely the time Chris saw so many cared for him. We believe this inspired him to write in his Life Lesson to *"cherish every moment"*. When Chris pushed his friends away, he realized how much he missed them.

Chris cherished the unique characteristics each person possessed. After he moved from Hawaii, he missed wrestling with his friends Ryan and Jimmy. He loved to be with fun-loving people and those who would do spontaneous and risky adventures.

It was important to Chris to be committed to his friends. But he also realized he could not have the fun-filled adventures he once had with his friends. He instead needed to commit time to pursue medical school. He realized he was going to have to choose, and his commitment was first and foremost, to attend medical school.

And what his words mean to us

Chris taught us the importance of having friends and family. For years, we wanted to retire in Florida. We loved the thought of warm winters and all the outdoor activities. Obviously we were thinking of what can we do to entertain and make ourselves comfortable instead of maintaining friends and family relationships back in Kansas. After retirement, we now want to move closer to our family in Kansas. After losing Chris, we continue to realize how much we miss him and how important family really is.

We also realize how fragile life is. We realize how important it is to spend as much time with friends and family you can. Someday these opportunities will be gone, never to return while on this earth. And they may be gone much, much sooner than you would expect. So Chris taught us to *"cherish every moment"* of the time we have with friends and family. Maybe this is what he was thinking when he wrote this Life Lesson.

> *2 Bear one another's burdens, and thereby fulfill the law of Christ. **10** So then, while we have opportunity, let us do good to all people, and especially to those who are of the household of the faith. Galatians 6:2, 10*

Chapter 31

Chris: Your greatest weakness is your temper. Even if it is unfair and it sucks- reacting badly will only hurt you.

Chris most definitely had a temper. This was his greatest weakness. However, an asset for him was that he recognized this and in most cases, he was able to control it. Chris often felt he was always having bad luck. He often stated he wondered why so many bad things happened to him. If anyone had the right to be angry at life, Chris most certainly had reason to be on that list of people.

The family did not see much of this temper in his later years. We do not know if he tried to control his temper, or he had fewer reasons to be angry. We suspect the Lord was showing Chris His grace and love and Chris was able to feel the Lord was guiding him.

Another reason we may not have seen his temper in his later years was Chris realized *"reacting badly will only hurt you"*. This Life Lesson was a self-reflection for Chris. Chris knew when you lose your temper, you say things you wish you could take back. When he reflected back on his anger, he saw it really hurt himself; not the person he was angry with. He knew anger and temper just cuts off the ties to communication. Misunderstandings happen and both parties become upset. Chris had finally learned losing control would not give him a release of his emotions.

To avoid anger, Chris learned to adapt to other people's communication style. Chris became sensitive to how his own communication style affected other people, so he adjusted accordingly his ways of communication. To accomplish this, Chris would listen to others more than he would talk. He would slow down to observe and reflect on their emotions rather than immediately jump in, respond or react to a situation.

And what his words mean to us

Reacting badly to situations will only hurt us. The character of Job in the Bible is a great example of how to react when things go terribly wrong. We will all be tested in our lives. How we react to those tests will show the character we have. In many ways like Job, Chris had a life filled with success, intelligence, handsome looks and great friends. Like Job, Chris's life was then quickly assaulted and devastated on every angle. Chris was losing everything; all of his dreams. Only with a life built on God, did both Chris and Job endure.

We need to have a faith in God that endures through all the bad times, because bad times will come. We need to analyze our lives and make sure our foundation is in the Lord. When (not if) we go through these bad times, we need to know God is enough. Having a temper tantrum or reacting badly will not reflect the character of Christ.

God did not explain the reasons to Job why these bad things happened to him. To my knowledge, God never explained the reasons to Chris why bad things happened to him. Likewise, God never explained to us why this tragedy happened in our lives. Like Job, we need to remember God is all we really ever need. When everything was stripped away after Chris died, we recognized our faith in the Lord was really the only thing we ever had. We cannot get angry and demand God give us the answers. We have God and that is enough. We do not deserve to know the details of His plans.

> *1 Then Job answered the LORD and said, 2 "I know that You can do all things, And that no purpose of Yours can be thwarted. 3 'Who is this that hides counsel without knowledge?' "Therefore I have declared that which I did not understand, Things too wonderful for me, which I did not know." 4 'Hear, now, and I will speak ; I will ask You, and You instruct me.' 5 "I have heard of You by the hearing of the ear; But now my eye sees You; 6 Therefore I retract, And I repent in dust and ashes." Job 42: 1-6*

Chapter 32

Chris: Don't obsess over things you can't change.

Chris experienced many trials in his teenage and young adult years. Chris had to learn to deal with these trials in his own way. Many times, no one was around to help him, or he would not let people into his life when he was going through the trials. We think Chris was saying in this Life Lesson one must recognize when you *"can't change"* the outcome. The die has been cast and one must live out the consequences or continue through the trial. When things happened to Chris, he recognized he should make every effort to not *"obsess over things"*. He recognized later in his life some things he just *"can't change"*.

Reinhold Niebuhr wrote in the Serenity Prayer:

God, grant me the serenity,
to accept the things I cannot change,
the courage to change the things I can,
and the wisdom to know the difference.

Chris had high standards. He had high standards for himself and he had high standards for others. Having high standards for oneself and for others can be a great asset, but it can also be a curse.

Chris would sometimes obsess over his failures. But he knew the only option was to stop obsessing about the mistake. This was not easy for him and this Life Lesson would help him deal with these issues and move in the right direction. Chris recognized some things he just could not change. He would often say: "Get over it, there is nothing you can do about it", and "move on and suck it up".

We believe at times Chris did obsess over things he could not change. He used this Life Lesson to remind himself he should not obsess over why things happened to him. He would say "the only thing you have control of in life is your response; we cannot do anything about the response of others". He realized the only way he could get through life was to trust in the Lord. He believed we needed to trust the Lord would work out things for the best and we need to lay the issues at His feet.

And what his words mean to us

My wife and I did a jail ministry on Tuesday nights while we lived in Geneva, Illinois. Each time we visited the inmates, we started with the Serenity Prayer. It is such a special prayer for inmates, but it really touches our hearts also. Like Chris was saying, there are many things we cannot change in our lives. And instead of obsessing over them, we need to accept them.

We have thought about this Life Lesson often. We have thought about all the things in our lives we wish we could change. But of course, we cannot change any of them. Instead, we need to look at the trials in life and let these trials make us "better". Most importantly, we cannot let the trials make us a "bitter". Chris taught us with all the mistakes we have made, we need to move on and not let our mistakes consume us.

Here is the full text of the "Serenity Prayer". This prayer is not in the Bible. It was originally written by theologian Reinhold Niebuhr in the 1930s or 1940s. Many of us only hear the first few lines we provided before. But the rest of the prayer is also very beautiful and meaningful. Read it slowly, meditate on it, and let it be meaningful to you also.

The Serenity Prayer
God grant me the serenity
to accept the things I cannot change;
courage to change the things I can;
and wisdom to know the difference.
Living one day at a time;
Enjoying one moment at a time;
Accepting hardships as the pathway to peace;
Taking, as He did, this sinful world
as it is, not as I would have it;
Trusting that He will make all things right
if I surrender to His Will;
That I may be reasonably happy in this life
and supremely happy with Him
Forever in the next.
Amen.

By Reinhold Niebuhr

Chapter 33

Chris: Stay in contact with those who helped you in your journey.

Even in a life that was short, Chris had a diverse and varied life journey. Chris's life had so many adventures. He had been all around the world. He experienced many high points in his life, but he also experienced some tragic low points. Even through all he experienced, he knew he should stay in contact with those who helped him through his life journey. Chris remembered those who had helped him at one point in time. He was so grateful to them because they came to help and encourage him when he needed them the most. He never wanted to forget what they had done for him.

Chris kept in contact with many of his professors, old classmates and army buddies. He made a tray of goodies for Midwestern University professors to tell them how much they had helped him. He would send care packages to his army buddies who were deployed in Iraq. He would constantly stay in touch with them so he would not lose contact and their friendship. He did not forget about the people who helped him in his journey just because he was now living apart from them in a different location.

As an example, Chris continued to stay close to the family of a girlfriend. The mother is enlisted in the Army and has often been deployed to Iraq requiring the children to stay with extended family. This family and Chris had a special relationship. He sent care packages plus emails and letters to the family. In 2006, Chris sent a letter to the mother and volunteered to take care of the children while she was deployed. Chris was a model friend.

Chris especially reached out to maintain contact with his grandmother. Chris called her most every week. He told her about his adventures and listened to how she was doing. They had a close relationship and his grandmother appreciated it so very much.

And what his words mean to us

We all need to remember how important our friends can be. Friendship has so many facets. It means being there when your friends need you. It means looking for ways to encourage them and thinking of their needs before thinking of our own. It is so easy to be passive about keeping friendships and just let time and those friendships pass by. It is critical to maintain contact with our friends, even after we may have moved thousands of miles away. If we do not put forth effort to maintain the relationships with our friends, they will soon become only friends we may send a Christmas card to once a year.

For great friendships to be maintained, we need to love our friends in a different way than seems normal in today's society. We need to love our friends sacrificially. We may understand about sacrificial love for our immediate family, but sacrificial love for our friends may be a new concept for many of us. We learned a major part of sacrificial love is to never be selfish. This involves thinking and loving others more than thinking of ourselves. If we choose friends for only how they can benefit us, we will rarely benefit from having a true friend. We need to value the needs of our friends more than our own needs. This is the beginning of sacrificial love and having a true friend. The perfect model is how Jesus demonstrated sacrificial love through washing the feet of His disciples and then laying down His life for them and for us.

We have found our best friends are the ones who have accepted us for who we are. They can accept us for all our imperfections and weaknesses. Our true friends will understand we are not perfect and we will always make mistakes. For us to be a true friend, we need to be quick to ask forgiveness and ready to be forgiving to others. We need to stick to our friends like a brother and they need to feel they can trust us. We need to have close friends with whom we can be open and they can open their feelings to us. But we need to be cautious. Being totally open with casual friends can lead to ruin.

True friends will build each other up emotionally, physically and spiritually. If we can do this, we will feel good whenever we are around our friends. We will not only be able to receive strength and encouragement from our friends, but we can give back as well. We need friends so we can talk together, cry together and laugh together. And if we need to have those hard conversations for correcting our friends, the times of trust and love we built will carry us through it. You may be the one person who can change your friend's heart.

Most of us have had difficult journeys. Hopefully, each of us has friends who stuck with us during those difficult times. We need to be loyal to those friends and remember them like they remembered us.

Greater love has no one than this, that one lay down his life for his friends. John 15:13

Chapter 34

Chris: Learn what makes someone mad and avoid it or try the things that help relieve it.

C hris was a strong-willed child in his toddler days and it lasted through his late teen years. We first learned he was a strong-willed child when he was about two years old. He definitely made his parents mad at times. We bought books to help us cope with and handle our strong-willed child. We do not think we ever succeeded. In contrast, Chris's sister was compliant and obedient. Why God gave Lloyd and Cindy two such different children will never be known. Some say this is God's little joke on parents.

The wonderful thing we found out after he died is this became one of Chris's Life Lessons. He understood how he needed to avoid making people mad. In his adult years he earnestly sought to try to learn what made someone mad and then tried to "*avoid it*" or "*try the things that help relieve it*". We saw Chris in his adult life become frustrated at times, but the traits of making his parents mad from his earlier life had vanished. After his death, we never heard any of his friends say Chris made them mad, or that he made others mad. It was quite the opposite. His friends said Chris was an encourager, the class clown, and he was always was thinking of other's needs.

People said he also thought of the needs of others he barely knew, or those he did not know at all. An example is his first email to his fellow medical school classmates at Midwestern University in 2010. It was an email introducing him to all the entering freshman class members. He wrote he had access to a pickup and volunteered to help move anyone who needed assistance to move and get settled into an apartment or the dormitory. We recall him asking us to borrow our pickup one August day, but he never mentioned why he wanted to borrow it. We only found out later from his classmates.

And what his words mean to us

We need to consider the feelings of others above our own feelings. This is more than just being considerate of others, but a deeper understanding of their wants, needs and personalities. To do this, we need to learn more about them and get to know them on a personal level. We not only need to avoid the things that made them mad, but find ways to encourage them and comfort them. We need to learn what drives them to be happy and what we do that may upset them. We need to humble ourselves and learn more about them. We need to put their feelings above our own.

This Life Lesson also says to *"try the things that help relieve it"*. This involves even more effort on our part. We need to try to relieve their pain and anxiety for whatever is making them mad or upset. We should reach out to others in order to make them happy. We will now need to put forth the extra effort to try to console them and comfort them, just like the Lord comforts us in our grief and troubles.

> *3 Blessed be the God and Father of our Lord Jesus Christ, the Father of mercies and God of all comfort, 4 who comforts us in all our affliction so that we will be able to comfort those who are in any affliction with the comfort with which we ourselves are comforted by God. 5 For just as the sufferings of Christ are ours in abundance, so also our comfort is abundant through Christ. II Corinthians 1: 3-5*

Chapter 35

Chris: Be kind to those who may seem different from you or not as intelligent.

Chris knew he was blessed with an ability to do well in school. But it did not come easy; he worked at it very hard. He had exceptional grades all through high school and undergraduate college. We know he was smarter than his father, mother and sister put together; at least it seemed that way. Chris was not only very bright, but he was very handsome and athletic. Every girl he dated was gorgeous and several fell in love with him. Chris had many, many things going for him. Match these with a warm heart and a funny personality, Chris was gifted in many ways. But we never heard him boast of his exceptional talents or natural abilities. We have not decided if he understood these blessings. Sometimes we believe he had to know, but sometimes we think he did not understand how much he had going for him.

Only the Lord knows where Chris developed such a caring attitude for so many different kinds of people. He believed so deeply he should be kind to those who were different from him and to those who were less fortunate.

And what his words mean to us

The important things in life are not what you keep and store in your possessions, but what you give away. To reach people, we need to reach out to them. Chris did not have a lot of possessions, so he gave his time to those who were less fortunate. After his death, he was not remembered for the possessions he accumulated. Instead, he was remembered for the impact he had on people's lives.

We often let our job or our possessions influence our perception about how important we believe we are. But one day each of us will likely retire from our work. And believe it or not, the company we worked for will go on just fine without us. Likely they will forget about us in just a few days or weeks. Therefore, we should not feel we are better than anyone else just because of our job status or education.

We are reminded we need to be kind to everyone, especially those who are different from us or have a different societal status. We need to remember in the Lord's eyes, He loves and values each one of us the same. Being kind to people who are "*different from*" us can help us come to know them better and help us to be a witness of the love of our Lord Jesus Christ.

When we face the truth, everyone is different. We are no better than anyone. We all have fallen short in our lives and deserve eternity apart from God. Only through the sacrifice of Christ on the cross, we can be forgiven and we can become a child of God. If we believe in Him, we have been given this privilege. For this reason, we need to reach out to everyone, especially those who are poor or less fortunate than we are. We need to know and remember it is the Lord who has blessed us. We cannot claim success on our own merit. In the Lord's eyes, He loves us all the same and we are no better and no more important than the poorest of the poor.

> *Be kind to one another, tender-hearted, forgiving*
> *each other, just as God in Christ also has*
> *forgiven you. Ephesians 4:32*

Chapter 36

Chris: Forgive people, but also don't be mean to them.

Chris needed to forgive people and let his hurts go. For Chris to have as one of his Life Lesson's to "*forgive people and do not be mean to them*" is astounding and especially meaningful. It would have been so easy for Chris to hold a grudge and be mean and spiteful to people who hurt him.

Chris acquired this important lesson in his adult life. We think he learned to have a forgiving attitude in order to survive. If he had not allowed himself to forgive others, it would have destroyed him inside. His Life Lesson was not only to "*forgive people*", but he added "*also don't be mean to them*". This implies to forget the hurts someone has caused you, move on and restore the relationship.

Chris understood how much God had forgiven him. Chris understood how God's infinite love and forgiveness could help him forgive others. God's love helped him forget and learn to love those who hurt him.

And what his words mean to us

It is important to forgive, but it is more important to learn "how" to forgive. At times, it may be easy to forgive someone, but then we hold a grudge or act coldly toward them. Chris intentionally added at the end of his Life Lesson *"and don't be mean to them"*. This is what we need to learn the most. To truly forgive someone, we also need to repair and restore the broken relationship we have with the person.

Jesus Christ is our perfect model of forgiveness. It is so hypocritical to say we have forgiven someone and then be mean to them. Even at the cross, Jesus Christ did not hold a grudge to the ones who whipped Him unmercifully and then nailed him to the cross. He both forgave them and loved them at the same time.

By worldly standards, the people who beat, mocked and tortured Jesus did not deserve forgiveness. But Jesus forgave them through His compassion, kindness and love. We need to learn forgiveness reaches out to even those who do not deserve our forgiveness and to those who did not request it.

> *13 bearing with one another, and forgiving each other, whoever has a complaint against anyone ; just as the Lord forgave you, so also should you. 14 Beyond all these things put on love, which is the perfect bond of unity. Colossians 3:13-14*

Chapter 37

Chris: Don't steer people in the wrong direction.

Chris realized he could influence people in a way most of us cannot do. After he died, we heard so many stories from his friends about how he constantly promoted and pushed them to be better. He wanted them to fulfill all they were capable of doing. He wanted them to set their goals high. Influencing others seemed to come easy for him. He had a leadership ability that must have come from his Army training.

Before Chris would counsel people, he thoroughly thought out what he was going to say. He did this so he would come across as encouraging them and not offending them. If he was talking to someone about a delicate situation, he was careful to choose his words wisely. He would tailor his words and counsel to the specific person. He seemed to know the correct way to approach someone. Chris would counsel them to choose to live their lives in a way they could be proud of.

Chris rarely did things the simplest way possible. He put forth every effort needed to do the proper job. Chris would encourage his friends to pursue the more difficult way of doing things, if this was the best course for them to take. Often the best path for your life is not the easiest way.

Chris was not afraid to challenge his friends if he believed they were headed in the wrong direction. For many of us, it is often easier to look the other way so as not to be confrontational, even if we know a friend is making the wrong decision. Chris would never do this. He felt it was his duty as a friend to counsel them and steer them in the right direction.

Chris would especially counsel his sister, Lindsey, to keep moving forward in the right direction. Chris wanted the best for her and he would constantly encourage and push her to fulfill what she was capable of. For example, Chris wanted Lindsey to finish college. Lindsey took his advice and received her Bachelor of Science 14 months after Chris died.

And what his words mean to us

We need to set a good example for our friends. One way to do this is to demonstrate our care and concern for them. We need to challenge and correct them if we believe they are headed in the wrong direction. We need to care enough that we will even risk hurting the relationship if we believe we should challenge them to take a better direction.

We also need to "*steer people*" so they will know our values. If we have a personal relationship with Jesus Christ, we need to let people know we are a man or woman after the heart of God. We need to influence others. We need to show them our faith in the Lord is important to us. We need to represent Christ everywhere we go. If we say nothing to our friends about our faith, we are being lukewarm and we do not show our commitment to the Lord.

In everything we do, we need to reflect the character of God. We need to honor God. We need to remember the impression people will have of Christ when they talk to us or are around us. Like this Life Lesson, we all have so many occasions where we could easily lead others away from the Lord and lead them down the wrong path. Sometimes we can allow others to stray down the wrong path by simply being quiet and not wanting to be confrontational. Like Chris, we need to resist taking the easy way out. We need to make every effort to steer our friends in the right direction.

> *16 Let the word of Christ richly dwell within you, with all wisdom teaching and admonishing one another with psalms and hymns and spiritual songs, singing with thankfulness in your hearts to God. 17 Whatever you do in word or deed, do all in the name of the Lord Jesus, giving thanks through Him to God the Father. Colossians 3:16, 17*

Chapter 38

Chris: Don't ever try to get revenge. If someone makes you mad, you have to let it go.

In Chris's short life he experienced great joys along with some difficult times. At first, it was a challenge for him to turn the other cheek when someone had hurt him or wronged him. But Chris saw his quest for justice when he was wronged should never turn into seeking revenge. Chris eventually saw in his life he needed *"to let it go"*. He believed when he reacted out of anger and plotted to seek revenge, it only hurt himself. Revenge can easily backfire and besides, it never solves anything. What we know from this Life Lesson is reacting in anger, carrying a grudge or trying to get revenge will never be satisfying. Chris knew he had to let go of these memories. He had to forgive. And if possible, he had to forget.

Chris sought constructive ways to deal with his hurts and painful memories. First and foremost, Chris prayed about his hurt. His other Life Lessons revealed his worshiping at his church for solace. He turned to the Lord and trusted Him for peace.

Secondly, Chris would occupy his mind with other things. He would remember his good times, his cherished memories and reflect how truly blessed he was. He would take long hikes to unwind and reflect on God's beauty in nature. Finally, Chris reminded himself he simply could not dwell on his hurts and memories. He just had *"to let them go"*.

<u>And what his words mean to us</u>

We should not seek revenge when someone has done us wrong. We need to show them either they did not offend us, or we have forgiven them. We need to be friendly to all people, even when they are unfriendly to us. Unfortunately, when we get hurt by someone, we can easily choose evil to try to settle the score. However, the Lord commands us to pay back people who have wronged us with good. Paying back someone who has wronged us with good can actually be more devastating to the person than seeking revenge. Being kind and generous may make their conscience burn.

It is God's job to make sure justice is done and people who wronged us get what they deserve. Said in another way, we should leave the wrong they have done to us to God. We may need to wait until we get to heaven to see how God's justice is done, but still it is God's job to accomplish. Only God can give us this kind of strength to love others and be kind and generous. Our job is to pray for them and make peace with everyone as much as possible.

> *17 Never pay back evil for evil to anyone.*
> *Respect what is right in the sight of all men. 18 If*
> *possible, so far as it depends on you, be at peace*

*with all men. **19** Never take your own revenge, beloved, but leave room for the wrath of God, for it is written, "VENGEANCE IS MINE, I WILL REPAY," says the Lord. **20** "BUT IF YOUR ENEMY IS HUNGRY, FEED HIM, AND IF HE IS THIRSTY, GIVE HIM A DRINK; FOR IN SO DOING YOU WILL HEAP BURNING COALS ON HIS HEAD." **21** Do not be overcome by evil, but overcome evil with good. Romans 12: 17-21*

Chapter 39

Chris: Don't judge others who are different than you and you do not know anything about.

Chris was not a judgmental person. He experienced a diversity of people in his life and he accepted others as they were. Chris saw so many people in so many different places. Each came from a different walk in life. He met the very rich and he met the poorest of the poor. While in the Army, he served and protected the people in devastated, war-torn Bosnia. He studied with multinational students in Hawaii. He experienced the poor and the weak when he visited slums in India, Mexico and Viet Nam. He was a summer intern at Duke University. Chris knew God gave him more than others, but Chris knew he was not better than others.

Chris was also a humble person. He was humbled when he realized how dependent he was on the grace of God and the peace that came from the Lord. Studying was extremely difficult during his medical school entrance exams and the exams he later had in medical school. It made Chris aware he was never going to accomplish becoming a doctor on his own merits; he needed the strength of God.

Chris never had a lot of material things. At one time in the Army, he drove a lime-green Ford Mustang. It was a pretty cool-looking car. But except for the Mustang, his cars typically had very high mileage, they were maintenance intensive and they were only worth a few hundred dollars. He did not wear trendy clothing. He was comfortable in his Hawaiian flip-flops, faded tee shirts and khaki shorts. He never wore a watch, a hat, sunglasses and he never had a tattoo. He wanted to give gifts to people instead of receive them. He never had a lot of money in the bank. When you have little, you have few things to brag about. When you have little to brag about, it is also harder to be judgmental of others.

With this as a backdrop, we never heard Chris say judgmental things of others. We believe Chris understood he was no better than anyone else. He believed everyone was different and unique in their own way. He knew just because others were different from him, did not make him better.

And what his words mean to us

Are you too critical of others? Instead of being judgmental and critical, we need to show love to others, show compassion to others and be merciful to others. As it says in Luke 6:37, if we do not judge others, they will not judge us. If we do not condemn others, they will not condemn us. Finally, if we forgive others, they will forgive us. If we treat others generously, we will receive generosity back from them. We are to love others and not be judgmental of them.

We should not stereotype others. It is easy to think we are better than someone because we have a better job or because we live in a better part of town. We should examine our motives when we are judgmental of others. Do we have the same faults we are being critical of in others? Maybe the things we want to change in others are the same things we need to change in ourselves. Do we magnify the mistakes in others when we make these same mistakes ourselves?

We need to continually remind ourselves, as Chris did, everything we have is by the grace of God. Everything we have does not even belong to us. It all belongs to God. If we have accepted Christ into our hearts, we are children of God. But even the right to be a child of God was not earned on our own merits; this too is a gift from God. With this said, we have no right to think we are better than anyone else.

When we next want to judge others, we first need to examine ourselves. Are our motives right? We now need to remember we need to be humble and remember all the things God has given us. We need to be loving and gracious to others. Instead of being critical, we need to reach out and help them. This is what Chris would have done.

> *37 "Do not judge, and you will not be judged; and do not condemn, and you will not be condemned; pardon, and you will be pardoned. 38 "Give, and it will be given to you. They will pour into your lap a good measure -pressed down, shaken together, and running over. For by your standard of measure it will be measured to you in return." Luke 6: 37-38*

Chapter 40

Chris: Don't be a part of someone else getting hurt.

All of us have been hurt by others. Chris was no exception. Because of this, Chris did not want to be a part of hurting others. He knew and experienced within his own life the pain of being deeply hurt. Being hurt by others left him worn and exhausted.

Chris would counsel his friends not to offend others or cause them pain. Chris had a roommate who was not being faithful to his girlfriend. Chris admonished his friend to be honest with her. When the girlfriend called the apartment, Chris was torn about covering for his roommate and being deceitful and untruthful. Chris did not want to "*be a part of someone else getting hurt*".

It seemed Chris saw the hurt in others and had a deep empathy for them. After Hurricane Katrina, he rallied his friends at Chaminade University to have a carwash so they could donate the money to the victims. When Chris saw someone being bullied, ignored or put down, he came alongside them to encourage them.

He often told us about his favorite countries when he cruised around the world during the "Semester on the Sea". He always spoke first about visiting and experiencing the poor in India and Vietnam. Chris could sense the hurts in others and took pleasure in encouraging them, acting silly to lift up their spirits, and finding ways to give them hope.

And what his words mean to us

We need to give our time and money to reach out to help those in need. Giving "lip service" about caring for someone is easy. Caring for someone who you do not know is different and a true act of humility.

Every year our church has a Sunday morning where we do not worship at the church building. Instead, we go out in groups and help those in need. In 2012, our group helped a single mother by fixing up her home. She has a daughter with MS and an elderly father living with her. She is barely making ends meet. She did even not attend our church. On this Sunday morning, instead of us dressing up in our Sunday clothes and going to church to listen to a sermon and singing songs, two of us fixed the toilets in her home, while others repaired other parts of the home. We spent four hours lying on her bathroom floor (which she forgot to clean) replacing the gaskets on the toilet bowls. We think, in a small way, this was a demonstration of what it really means to humble ourselves and care for someone like Jesus would have wanted us to do. Our church calls this: "having people see Jesus with skin on".

Jesus Christ was humble and He served. He gave up His rights by coming to earth, living among us and then giving up his life as a ransom to save us. Like Christ, we need to demonstrate a servant's attitude. We do not want to serve others so we can get something back from it. Instead, we want to serve others so they can see a servant's heart and someone who really cares for them.

> *3 Do nothing from selfishness or empty conceit,*
> *but with humility of mind regard one another as*
> *more important than yourselves ; 4 do not merely*
> *look out for your own personal interests, but also*
> *for the interests of others. 5 Have this attitude*
> *in yourselves which was also in Christ Jesus,*
> *Philippians 2: 3-5*

Chapter 41

Chris: Try not to judge others. You haven't walked in their shoes.

C hris believed each of us has our own styles in life. Chris never wanted to judge someone simply on their outward appearance or stereotype someone on a first impression. Therefore, Chris did not want to judge them just because they were different.

Chris knew he had his own faults. He was fully aware others had likely gone through difficult times as he had. Chris realized he should not judge others because he had not gone through the same trials, tribulations and events they had experienced. Said in another way, he had not *"walked in their shoes"*. Therefore, He wanted to know someone before he formed conclusions about them.

And what his words mean to us

Unfortunately, many of us find pleasure in finding faults in others. We seem to relish tearing others down. We need to remember how painful and hurt we feel when someone else is judging us unfairly. Instead of judging others, we need to examine our motives. The criticisms and weaknesses we find in others are likely the same faults we possess also. The same things we want to change in others are the things we need to change in ourselves. Before we start to criticize someone else, we need to first examine ourselves to see if our actions merit the same judgment. Then instead of judging, we need to show love and compassion to the person and forgive them if they have harmed us.

> *Do not judge so that you will not be judged.*
> *Matthew 7:1*

Chapter 42

Chris: Don't be arrogant or opinionated. Accept and praise other's opinions.

Chris was a humble person. When he took a group to go mountain climbing, he would walk alongside the slowest member of the group to encourage him and build up his esteem. He tried to make anyone and everyone feel included, welcome and valuable, no matter who they were.

In his later years it would be rare Chris would openly contradict others or be argumentative if he held another opinion. He wanted others to understand he valued their opinions and he was listening and considering their views. If he then disagreed with someone, he would then simply and politely offer another opinion or a different perspective.

Chris had a hard time accepting praise from others. Even when others tried to compliment him, we could tell he seemed to discount or dismiss their admiration. Whether he simply did not believe what was said or did not want to show pride by accepting the praise, we will never know.

And what his words mean to us

We need to honestly and accurately evaluate ourselves. Some of us overestimate ourselves and fall into becoming "*arrogant or opinionated*". Some of us think too little of ourselves and as a result we have low self-esteem. If we value or rate our success or achievement by worldly standards, we will always be disappointed. There will always be someone we envy who is more attractive, has more money, or has a better job.

Instead, we need to focus on God and understand how He sees us and values us. Only then can we set aside the standards of this world and wholly and completely offer ourselves in service to Him. If we confess our sins, identify ourselves with Jesus Christ and put our trust in Him, God forgives our sins. We then have the privilege and full status of being God's children. This is when we begin to spend eternity with Him, both here on earth and eventually in heaven.

> *For through the grace given to me I say to everyone among you not to think more highly of himself than he ought to think; but to think so as to have sound judgment, as God has allotted to each a measure of faith. Romans 12:3*

Postlude

One evening in February, 2012, I was granted a dream in my sleep from the Lord. In the dream was a vision of a beautiful meadow with a narrow, paved, winding road. I was standing just outside the curvature of the road where it made a U-turn and the road once again continued back in the direction away from me in the direction from which it came. Along the road was a meadow with beautiful and bright yellow, red and blue flowers. The flowers were surrounded by lush, dark green grass. The cloudless sky was a brilliant, bright blue. The place was so strikingly beautiful it almost seemed like a scene right out of the movie *The Wizard of Oz.*

After a short time, a shimmering, white wagon pulled by two white horses approached me on the road from a distance. I recall admiring how beautiful the wagon was. It had three rows of seats. The white paint on the wagon seemed to glimmer and sparkle. The wagon pulled up slowly from the left and stopped in front of me at the curvature of the road. I did not understand what the wagon was doing even though I noticed a few were already sitting in the front and middle seats of the wagon. I also noticed someone older was driving the wagon and instructing those already sitting. I call this person the "wagon master", because he was definitely in charge of those in the wagon and where it was going.

Soon, Chris and a few others walked up from behind me. Chris looked so happy. He was laughing and talking to the others like he knew them. Then the wagon master looked directly at Chris and called to him. He quietly said "come and get into the wagon, it is time to go Home". I instantly knew the wagon was coming to take those in the wagon to heaven to be with God. Chris walked past me and got into the back row of the wagon right behind the others who were already sitting in the wagon. They turned around and told Chris how happy they were to be in the wagon and how happy they were to see Chris coming along with them.

As I watched Chris, he was quiet. He continued to have a big grin on his face. He looked at me and seemed to be at such peace. He seemed so restful. He seemed so anxious, but at the same time he had a calmness which expressed his utter joy and tranquility. He quietly sat in the back and did not say a word. He once again looked at me and I saw on his face a joy much like the face of a child on Christmas morning.

I did not recognize the others who walked up with Chris. All I recall about them is the wagon master who told Chris to get into the wagon also told the others it was not their time. The wagon master told them they would need to wait until the wagon returned someday. He assured them he and the wagon would come back.

Then the wagon master got into the wagon and slowly drove on down the road, this time heading away from me. I continued to watch the back of Chris's head as the wagon drove away. In a few moments, it traveled over the hill and I did not see it again.

This was truly a gift from God. He was showing me He was taking Chris home. I too could now be at peace. It was Chris's time to go home, but others, like me, needed to stay behind for the time being. Someday, it will be our time for the wagon master to call us to get into the wagon. And someday, we hope the wagon master will call you to get into the wagon to go to be with God in heaven. If you trust and believe in the Lord and have confessed and turned from your sins, we firmly know you have a reserved seat.